Other books by JEAN MARIE RUSIN

Spooky
Willow Lakes HAUNTING
NIGHT OF TERROR
A POLISH CHRISTMAS STORY WITH A MAGICIAL
CHRISTMAS TREE
A DRAMA QUEEN COLLIDE WITH PRINCE CHARMING
NO ENDING DREAMS
GERMANY INVADED POLAND SEPTEMBER 1, 1939 MY LIFE
STORY
MYSTERIOUS NIGHTS SÉANCE AND GHOSTLY HAUNTING
THIN ICE ZOMBIES IN LA NOWHERE TO HIDE
LADY ROSE
LUST LOVE SEX PLEASURE
NO ENDING DREAMS REUNION
NO ENDING DREAMS SECRETS
Thin Ice Zombies In LA Nowhere to run or hide! RETURNS!
Broken Bridge Lies body of Water

Coming soon!!!
Thin Ice Zombies IN LA Nowhere to run or hide! BATTLE.

Long Silky Blonde Girl

Jean Marie Rusin
Edited by K. Downing

authorHOUSE®

AuthorHouse™
1663 Liberty Drive
Bloomington, IN 47403
www.authorhouse.com
Phone: 1-800-839-8640

While this story was inspired by true events and recollections of the author, the names and relationships of those involved have been changed or altered to protect their identity

First published by AuthorHouse   11/1/2011

ISBN: 978-1-4670-6877-2 (sc)
ISBN: 978-1-4678-3599-2 (e)

Printed in the United States of America

Any people depicted in stock imagery provided by Thinkstock are models, and such images are being used for illustrative purposes only. Certain stock imagery © Thinkstock.

This book is printed on acid-free paper.

Photo by Deborah T Kilday

Loving memory
Gary J. Stagliano
Nov 14, 1951 to April 23, 2003

Dedicated too my DAD.
WlADYSLAW RUSIN
MARCH 21, 1921 AND JULY 8, 2010.

Early years

My mom and dad were born in Poland and went they were teenagers and the German invaded Poland and the Germans came into Poland to find workers and they took my mom and dad from there home and my grandmother begged them to let my mom to stay, but the German soldier said no, we need workers and they took my mom my and my mom was looking back at the door and they walks her into the truck and ever since that day, my mom didn't sees her mom again, and about my dad, they drove up with the truck and they stop at his home and they took him away from his family too, and then they didn't know where they were going to unknown location, and when they arrival to the train station and they had to get off the truck and go into single lines, and some when into another truck and my mom and dad at different time enter the train to unknown, and they receive a piece of bread and water for there journey. So my dad said that he had a good farmer, and he was able to go places, one time, my dad was dating a German girl and he got caught and they only when to the movie and he almost got killed and my dad said, but he was send back to the farmer and then there was time that my dad was working in the field, and a German car came up and told my dad to bring some a blanket from the barn so, my dad snuck out of the barn and ran the other direction and then they started to shoot at him, but my dad did not get hurt and escape into the woods and hide out, and then couples days later, my dad was safe and when back to the farmer, and there was another time that the German caught my dad and they started to beaten him up and about that time he was about seventy pound and lucky that his farmer found him and at that time my dad thought he was going to died but my dad got better and when with the farmer and then he was healthy and strong and was

1

able to work at the farm, but my dad told me that he saw the bomb falling and a lot of his friends died and he said that he was lucky, and now about my mom she worked for a woman name Amelia and she had a mean son that called my mom a swine, and my said to him the same, and one time my mom reported to the authority, they wanted to take her away and the Amelia, and she plead and my mom stay until the war was over and then the America came and Amelia said, there is a black man and you hide and he will hurt you, but my mom was afraid and hid and then in couple days the America took my mom to the barrack and met more polish peoples and one time she met my mom and the war was over and then they started to date and then they got married and then in Feb 1949 my sister was born and then about two year later, my dad said to my mom that he was going to America to find work, so my sister and my mom stay in Germany and then my dad got a job at tobacco and then a job at a carpet place and then few month later, my mom and sister would coming to America, and then my sister got measles and the trip got delay and then my sister got better and they were on there ways to America and then my mom step on the ship and she got sea sick before the ship sail and the captain said you poor child, and my mom and sister when to there room and then one day my sister fell but she didn't get hurt, and all the ways to America, my mom was sick and meanwhile my dad was working at Thomasville, ct and work very work and live in a rooming house, one room and kitchen at a polish woman and share the kitchen, and then when my mom and sister came to American and they arrival to New York City and my mom and sister took the train to Berlin, Ct and then my dad was waiting for my mom and sister to arrival and then my dad took my sister to there new home and they didn't understand the language, and a new country and then they lives there for a while and then they live there about one year and then they got a different apartment a and it was not easy to find a place with children, because the landlord didn't accept that very much and then in December 1952 my brother was born and they move into a different place and then they belong to Holy Cross church and about two year later. My parents didn't have a car and they walks to church with my sister and my brother and then they move to Broad street where I was born and then my sister started school at Sacred heart school and then,

I was born in New Britain General Hospital on July 31 to the Parents of Walter and Marcella and I visited the doctors a lot because I was a sick child and when time went by there was incident that I almost died, but our neighbor Tina told my parents to take to the emergency room and my parents didn't speak no English and they didn't understand what the doctor was saying, but that one doctor said to my parents was just give her aspirin and I will be fine in the morning but the neighbor step in and said we need to take her now, because she is a very sick girl and she need it now, because she might died and so Tina drove my parents to the hospital and I was in my mom hands and then when they arrival into the emergency room the nurses and doctors check me out and one of the doctor is name was Dr. Brother, and the doctor said that Jean had a small windpipe and we need to make it bigger and than, also Dr. Brother said she will be lucky to make it to her second birthday, and but at this point my parents didn't understand what the doctor said, and time when by and I once again I was at the hospital again, but that night I snuck out of the crib and walks in the hallways and so one of the nurse, caught and told the doctor and they put a net over the crib and then I was calling out and saying I hate you I want to go home now.

So my parents came to visit me and I had to stay there one more days and I cried and stomp my feet, and then the next days I was going home.

But I was still seeing the doctor in his office and he was taking blood test and they took from my finger and I didn't like it very much.

When I was a little baby about eight weeks old my mom when to work has a housekeeper at that time my dad was laid off from the factory and we would living on broad street in New Britain, Connecticut, and in that place we didn't have no hot water or a bathtub, so when I was a little baby my mom gave a bath in the kitchen sink and at that times they didn't have bathtub or shower in the apartment in the 1950's. But my mom told me that we had a steel bathtub and my mom had to heat up the water on the stove.

Also I have an older sister and her name is Mary and a brother is the middle child and his name is Walter, and he is deaf. I also played with my brother and learned sign language, and I am the only one that know sign language in my family and my mom and dad and sister don't know it well but my dad and my sister know a little bit but I know more.

But I need to say that my parents came from Germany and they work for the Germans during World War 2. There was time that my dad didn't know that he was going to make it and but his farmer help and he got better.

So back to me well, I was not a healthy child and I always ended up in the hospital, and the hospital bills were a lot of money that they didn't have much but in time they paid the bills, but I visited a lot doctor appointment and getting a lot of poking on my finger, and also the doctor said it I make it too my second birthday and I would lives.

At this time I pass my two year old birthday and then I was about four year old and ,my sister and brother took me to my godmother house and then somehow I just mange to leave on my own and ended up in a police man arm and he took me to my house and my parents were surprise at the door it was I and an Police man, and he said I saw your child walking on the sidewalk and I asked her and she told me that she wanted to comes home, so then the officer asked who was watching her? But at that time the police officer, didn't say anything but left me with my parents.

Later that day my sister and brother came into the house and said where is Jean, well my mom spoke in polish and said she came home with a policeman and said, and my mom said how were you watching your sister?

Well my sister said well I got distract and so I didn't sees her when she when, but we will still living on broad street and my dad had a green Buick and it was a 1955 model. But one day when my dad was driving the car, somehow my sister just somehow opens the door and almost fell out.

At that point my dad yells at her and said, don't do this again, but in polish language and my sister said I will not do it again, and it never happened again, and now I was getting a little older and soon I will be started school and my parents now belonged to Sacred Heart and I started school at a catholic school and I knew that I cried the first day and also pee in my pant.

Some of the children were making fun of me and the nun called my parents and said your daughter pee on the first day of school and what wrong with her? Well my mom said it was only an accidentally, but the nun refuse to listen.

I when to that school up to the second grade and then I when to Burritt school and I had a teacher name Miss Katz and she was nice sometime and then sometime she put me into the corner, and punished me, for no reason at alls but she pick on me a lot.

But I only when there for a year and then I got transfer to Smalley school and I really didn't like that place it was dark and dim and the kids were means too me.

About two month later I went to Benjamin Franklin and I went up to fourth grade and then I left that school and I once again attend Sacred heart school but some of the friends I knew like Janet but once again the kids make fun of me and then I stay about two years and then I left that school and I went to Nathan Hale, now I am in Junior high and before that we move to Washington street and it was a better place to lives and then my parents make friends and they had party and it was a good place to lives.

I also belonged to a drum crop with my friend Elise and I went to practice and March in the band. But I also when for guitar lesson and teacher said I have short finger to play that instrument, so I stay for a while than I quit. Also I belonged to the brownie and then Girl Scout and it was fun and met new friends and going out like meeting at the park for the Girl Scout meeting.

Time when by and then couple years later, we move into that house that I live now and it is off Slater road, and it is a nice house.

But from Washington street when we move into the new house I still attended the same junior high school and sometime my dad drove me to school or I took the Farmington Ave to school with my friends Betty Lou and Alma, and that was for a while. But before we move to the house, went I lives at 204 Washington street I hang out with Elise, Dawn and Brain, and sometime I also eat dinner at there home and they also came to my house to eat and plays game, and then we went to places like to Battery Park and we walks there and it was more than a mile and it was a lot of fun. But need to talked about the time when I was a little child in the carriage that my mom and dad when to Walnut hills park and my sister and brother too, and we spend a lot times together.

Also my parents had a lot friends and we when to a lot of birthday party and they took pictures and it was a good times. Then we when to the beach with our neighbor and they also had party in the backyard and it was a goodtime.

Some of my parents were polish and Italian and they got along fine.

But there was time that we got a puppy but we couldn't keep that puppy and it was name "Blackie" but the landlord was means and my parents had a choice to keep the dog and move out or give to there friends and stay in that apartment, well I must tell you that my parents gave the dog away and we alls cried and one day my brother found a kitty and he bought it home and my dad said tell that cat and I don't want it here and my brother to his friend Tommy, and that was the end of the pets.

Then there was incident that there was a wild cat on the edge of the window that my dad fight with the cat at that time, he was lucky that he didn't get scratch or bitten probably would have Rabies and that was the end of it.

Then there was an other incident in that apartment, that there was a air condition fire and the firemen came and it was fine but I when to bed and my mom I stay in the living room but I think I did a stupid thing going back to bed when it was not safe yet, and then one night that my sister heard sound and noises from the outside and inside of the apartment, because that place was haunted, because one man jump from the third floor and it was a really scaring place to live, and now my friends when back to the park and we climb over the fence to the courant camp and we walks around and then we walks back and then time when by and everyone would getting older and started to hang out with different peoples and then we move to the house and but I was not too happy about that, but I met new friends, like Bernadette and Diane and Skipper and Jane, and Elaine and Robert, and Geoff, at first seem like they were nice, but every times when I went over to play they started to make fun of me, this was in 1966, and my parents bought the house on Howe Road and it was a nice place and then my dad friends help us move to that house, so that night, went my dad went to work, my mom and my sister and I slept in the same bed and we would afraid of the new house and the noise of the creak and the heater, and that was only for one night.

The next night my sister and I slept upstairs and my mom and dad slept downstairs, and then my sister got her own phone in her room and the phone with the chimes, and it was a nice sound and a princess phone.

Also my sister was in her last year of high school and refuse to go Pulaski so she kept going to New Britain High school and graduate in 1967.

My sister also when to the prom with her boyfriend Robert and then my sister makes dinner like lobster and steak and salads.

About three year later my sister got married to Robert and they had the wedding at Sacred Heart church and my sister was working at FAFNIR Bearing. The reception at wonder bar in Newington, and I was a bride maid, and at that time I was going through panic and nervous time that I really couldn't stand being in the same place long.

But I was fine and my sister when on the honeymoon and they came back I make a cake for them, but they were lucky that they missed the first plane because it crash because of a storm, but they still had a shaking plane going to Bermuda, but they were safe.

So let me tell you about my friends that I hung out with, so I will start with Bernadette and Diane and they thought they were smarted than I and they started to talks behind my back. And laughing in front of me, because I didn't have prefect teeth and thought I was not normal.

But we also plays kick ball and hang out and they also had pool and I was not allow just one of us so I was watching and then rest were swimming in the pool and then sometime I when over and we watched a some TV.

Now I will go to the boys, like Geoff, so he was the first boy that kissed me in his tree house, and then like Gary and Robert and Mary and Susan we plays touch football and on Sunday we went to the Memorial hospital and visit the patience and about one hour on Sunday and then I met Jane and one day she hit me and stole a record from me and she was a fresh girl.

Now about the boys I spent a lot of time at Geoff house and there was his step brother Gary but a foster child, and then Bobby and Eddie, so one night I when over there and they decided to trap me there so, they tight me up and use a stick and tried to have sex with me so my mom decided to go and get me so when my mom arrives they let me go and then I when home and my sister wanted to called the police. But my sister didn't call the police.

Then the second incident happened, at Bobby and Eddie house and I got out ok too. There was a time that my parents went to a wedding and I was home with my dog "Sammy" and I black man came to the door and my dog and I hid in the closet until he left and I told my parents about that I was really scare and but only happen once and I didn't forget. And there was a time that my father took his friends to find a Christmas tree and we got lost and we were like on high bridge and water on the bottom and I told my dad to turn around but at that time we had to keep on that bridge and then somehow we ended up in the woods and we turn around and headed back on that road and we took those peoples home and we were safe.

Also went I was going to Nathan Hale, some of classmate were the same and they wanted to hurt me, but I cannot forget what happen in the Franklin School and how that Black girl tried to have sex with me in the bathroom some how she grab me and somehow she touch me in the wrong ways and I won't forget that day.

But I didn't tell anyone until now because I was afraid and ashamed what happened to me. In school there was a lot incident that I would like to forget, there were some guys grabbing me in the classroom and they turned off the light and they were chasing me in the classroom.

Now I will tell you about one of my friends told me to meet Bob, and I thought he like me but he wanted to have sex with me, so he took me to falcon field in the bushes and told me to give him a blow job and I was force to do so.

Also he wanted to sees him a lot so I refuse and then I haven't seen him.

So I need to tell you that one day I was walking back from the library and I just didn't remember where I lived and I got scares.'

Well I was a not a good girl because I did skip school and lies about it but went my parents find out I got punish and my dad took out his belt and hit me and never again I didn't skip school and that was in my freshmen year and also the principal said if you want to quit school or stay you need to decided and he talked with my parents.

After that I didn't skip school or I when to school and I got my good grades and then I decided to take driving lesson but I fail the course and I waited until I graduation from High school and my dad was the teacher and I pass the driving test and I drove the car and then I got a job at Caldor for inventory, and my best friend from high school was Bonnie.

Barbara and I when bowling with friends Jim and other friend to the bowling place in Newington and before that time I met Frankie and Patty, and Patty was a friend that I met in school and one more time I skip school and she had sex with a black guy and his friend wanted from me but I said no.

But there was an other incident happened that I almost got shot but I was lucky that I didn't not, and it were been Patty fault, and the first guy that I did have sex with was Frankie, he was Patty friend.

Time when by and he came over with Patty and we all hang out.

When they took me home they walks through the cemetery and I refuse and scare. About one year later I didn't sees they and Patty mother accuse me being a bad influence in her daughter and we stop seeing each other again.

So I make new friends and me also graduation from High school.

Year 1970's

In 1970 my parents had an automobile accident it was a head on collision and my mom when to Hartford hospital and then, and before that my sister got married in October 3, 1970, and so I was saying that my mom had a head injure but she was fine that day I almost went but I decided to stay home.

My mom when to a lot doctors and therapy and they help her.

In 1973 I graduation from high school and I hang out with Barbara B and we when places and I also visit her and she came to my house.

In December 1977 I met Ricky in G. Fox went my brother and I would playing Pac man, and Ricky introduce himself and I did too and then we exchange phone number and then Rick started to comes over my house and we watched the "Time Machine" and we when to sees the movie airport 1977 and we also when too a lot of beaches and we when to walnut hill park and I ran into my friend Mary from school. Also Ricky taught me the electric slide and we like the singer Leo Sayers. The song dance the night away, and I floating in his arms, all night long and he make me happy.

But she was jealousy that I was with this handsome man and she and her mother didn't like it and we ran into them at "Walnut Hills Park" top of the hills and near he pool. And Ricky and I played ping pong, and playing pool in the basement and we also make love, and Rick make dinner at his house and we took walks together and at that time I was very negative about myself and I felt that I didn't like myself, so let guys used me for sex and especially Ricky, but at that time I felt that I was in Love with him and he just wanted to be my friend but I think at that time I wanted more from him than he offer me. So I felt that he was good for me and so

I did have sex with him a lot and I was not lonely. But he was not my first boyfriend and at that time I still saw Frankie and he also used for sex and we walks to the park, and so I just was used. So Ricky and I and my mom and dad when to Picnic to Fafnir at the Berlin Fair ground and it was a good times and we had good foods and Rick really likes it and after the picnic we when home and later that day we order a large pizzas, at town and country, on Farmington Avenue, in New Britain, Ct and Ricky stay long until morning, and left home and the next morning my mom notice that twenty dollars was missing and my dad called up Ricky and accuse him, and later that day, they apologize to Ricky, because they just misplace the money. Well there was a time that Ricky and I when to Walnut hill park and he gave me a joint to smoke and I sprain my ankle and was unable to walks that happened twice and then one time I when to the hospital and they gave me a pain killer and I was fine.

Then there was an incident that I told my mom and dad that I was going clothes shopping, and I just somehow took a bus to New York city, but at that time I had to called my mom collect and told her where I was, and she told me to take the next bus home and I did.

But I really don't know why I did that? But I came home and nothing bad happened to me. So one day Ricky called me if I wanted to go to the beach on the Fourth of July and I said no and ever since than I didn't sees him until I told him about my girlfriend Bonnie, my best friend from High school.

One day Bonnie told me that she met some of my friends and she wanted to meet Ricky and I told her his phone number and they met and dating for a while and then I started to get some weird phone called and name calling so I had to change my phone numbers, and at that time I ran into my friend Don and Ann and they came over swimming at my house and than he broke up with her and he started to sees me and for a while and he move to Florida.

But Rick and I shared some beers and we got away about getting free pizza but once we didn't and so we didn't do that again and we stop seeing each others. Also, a friend Robert came around lunch and a friend George said why do always come here during lunch and ever since than. But he really likes Barbara B, and but one time he went Riverside and got me a bull for a gift. Also Robert was in the army.

Than my friend was moving to Florida and that was the last time that I saw him and than I got a job at "Smith and Gates and work over two year and half and than peoples were making fun of me and someone knew me that I knew her daughter in High school., and thought I was not normal and than I got sick and got panic disorder and I was not able to work and but I when back to that factory and than I got laid off and looked for work but I was not successful, and but no luck and then, but I kept on looking but I somehow kept on writing and but I never didn't finish anything at that time. I remember the time that my mom ended up in the hospital when she cut her hand, and she had to go to emergency. But they stitch her hand but was unable to go to work and because she was a housekeeper and she couldn't use the water because of the stitches, and then when she was better she did go back and than when my dad was working and he was stuck in the bizarre and he had to sleep at work and he drove up the hill in Pontiac Catalina, and up the snow and he came home.

There was a incident that someone knock at the door and it was a man and my dad let him in and I was scare and I was ready to runs out of the front door to get the police but he was a nervous man and walking back and forward and my brother said my father was stupid to let a complete stranger in the house, and than my sister was working at "Fafnir and there were bus tour to New York and we when to sees plays like "Hello Dolly" and other plays and than my mom and I would sick with a bad cold and it was not a good day to go there, but before that I had my tonsil remove and than about two year later my sinus operating, and so I didn't go that time.

It was fun time but I was always had some kind of fear and the last plays it really terrify me because of the height, and I was not feeling well and my mom neither. There was a time that my parents there friends had an anniversary party and they alls jump in the pool and they were yelling and screaming and eating soup, in the rain.

1980's year good and bad

In 1980 I didn't have no boyfriend and I was alone and I was not too happy about myself and I still didn't have a good job but than I when to get into some kind of program, so they told me about the construction workshop and they said they would give me test about colors and shape and so I said to myself why not! I when there a few times and then they wanted to meet my mom and said your daughter does not know the color orange and red, but I do know my colors but they didn't listen what I was saying and I told that woman that one day I will open up a business and she said "YOU" and I said yes, but I still kept on writing and than my sister said she was going to have a baby and I was exciting and so were my parents and my brother.

Also something was good that I wrote a query letter to an agent and he called me and he wanted to sees my work. So I did send my work and he didn't hear from him again. So I got upset and gave up on writing again!

Then I attended computer school and I met new friends and I graduation in Data Entry and so I when to looked for work at Allstate and Otis company but I didn't get hire. In 1980 my nephew was born his name is Johnny and everyone was very happy and then my sister asked if I wanted to be a godmother and I said no because I really didn't feel right and shaking and nervous, so she pick her friend Patty and my brother for godparents.

Ands about four year later Ronny was born and that was in 1984, and that year I met Jon and his aunt Heather came over and I just came out of the pool and we started to talked and exchange phone and so he was on his ways to Los Angeles for Law School, so when he got there he gave me a called and we talked for hours and so we talked about getting together

12

and than in the year of 1985 I when to Los Angeles, California and move in with Jon and than, I got a job at CBS and it was a exciting job and so Jeff took me every morning to the farmer market and than I walks to the studio and than I met Dick Clark and the peoples that work there.

Also one day I also won a radio but I probably should not because I work there but I did and I kept the radio in Jeff and mine apartment.

But I did called my parents a lot and I did go back to Connecticut and flew back to LA, after the visit with my family.

Then Jon pick me up from the LAX and drove me home and one time the San Anna winds and it really got dark and at night it was cold.

Sometime I make breakfast and sometime Jon did and but Jeff stay up long study his law books to do study.

One day Jon took me to the Beverly center so I bought sweaters and dresses.

I also had lunch and I also took tour to the Chinese Theatre, walks of fame and the stars home.

I also went to the universal studio and met the gorilla and how the ride was a little scaring and but I was fine.

Then I took the bus back to the farmer market and walks around and looked at puppies and then Jon came and took me home and then we stop at the Beverly center and then we went to sees a movie "Moonstruck" and then we had dinner and we drove through a lot traffic and when we got home Jon hit a car in the garage, and we both walks inside the halls and Jon didn't leaves a note or anything.

About two hour later, I change and when to bed and Jon stay up and studying his law books and practice speaking to the mirror and then about 2 am Jon turn off the lights and when to bed, that Jon Place and mine had a lot cockroaches, and Jon spray a lot of times, and seem like they were gone but somehow there were more, and I couldn't leave soda open otherwise they would have when into the soda, somehow they really terrify me.

About a month later I took a flight to Connecticut and my brother and I had planned to go to Fort Lauderdale, I stay about a week and then I went back to LA to my boyfriend Jon and my brother took a other flight to Connecticut.

When I landed in Los Angeles waited for me at the terminal, and I walk by Jeff and he called out my name, and then we when to get the suitcase and then we when into the car and headed in traffic bumper to bumper. When we got home he put on the TV and then he asked me if I was in the mood for sex and I said ok! About a minute later we would making love and then the phone rang and he stop and answered it and it was his dad, Don.

So Jon talks with his dad for a while and then I got dressed and later that night I called my mom and dad and told them I am ok.

I also asked how they were.

But, I didn't stay on that long but I just wanted to hears there voice, it make me very happy and when I didn't I was sad.

Later that night Jon and I took a shower and he wash my body and I wash his and he carry me to the bed and told me to write a story and you were be able "think of one" so I did, then I started to rate him how he treated me.

One day Jon pushes me down on the fall and at that moment I started to feel a little dizzy and I asked him to hold me, but he didn't paid attention to me.

But Jon did apologize to me and I forgave him, and about two weeks later we when to a concert and we went for dinner like in a train car and it was really exciting, and then I order something from the menu and than so did he.

After dinner he paid for the meal and now we were headed to the concert and I was very happy, but at that time of my life I was a lot in the negative.

Then after the concert we headed home but Jon got lost and so we ended up not on the freeway but on the back road and I was really scared.

About one hour later, we got home and he drove in the garage and parks the car and we went inside and close the door and Jon put on heat.

Jon asked me if I wanted some coffee and I said " no thanks" and I change and went to sleep and I didn't know when Jon when to sleep but the next morning I saws Jon staring at me and smiling at me and I said why are you looking at me? Jon said well I just wanted to sees how you were sleeping.

Well I need to tell one month I thought I was pregnant but it was a fault alarm but I got my period, and I was relief but that time when I took a trip with my mom in April and we when to Hawaii.

On the flight to Hawaii and my mom said, looked at that snow up here but it was the clouds, and then my mom is I stupid, it cannot be snow.

Then every times when the plane went up my mom pick a magazine and then when the plane was level, my mom started to talk with me.

When we started too landed I hold my mom hands and I was a little scare, but that was not my first time flying. When my brother and I landed in Hawaii, I couldn't believe it and so that day, we were exhausted and so they had a greet place and they gave us breakfast and told us about tours that you can take In Hawaii and so my brother wanted to take a helicopter but I was a bit scare and so we didn't go but we took a boat tour that took about four hour and we saw our hotel from the boat, and the name of the boat was JADA, and you could even sees Diamond head from the boat and my brother when scuba diving in the deep water in the ocean, and I was worry about him at that time, and when I told my parents about it, they thought I was kidding around but I didn't, I did get on the boat and I am afraid of water. When you step into the ocean, seem like you are sinking and you don't want to go further, so you stay at the edge of the water unless someone is holding you and then you go into the water, then you sees the white sand and a beautiful view and you can go swimming in the pool, spa and lay in the sun, and the night you sees the ships sail in the night and you sees the lights on those ships and then you can dance all night long but watching TV, nothing good to watched, and then the next day we took a tour to North shores and so that beach is on the bottom and you have to do down to reach the beach and then you can feeds alls kind of fishing and you go into the water with white bread and you feed the fishes, and after that you get a lunch like potatoes salad and Marconi salad together, and then there an other tours that you can sees the water falls and Peoples jumping from the falls into the water, and then you can take a picture near the fall, and then after that when on another tour to the ice creams and the pineapple ice cream and I couldn't finish and later that night I order a pizza and it was really big and a lot time we when to the restaurant in the hotel and once in while at MC Donald, and that was good too and there was a time that we had Barbue Rib and it was good.

But I did call Jon and told him that I was having a wonderful time with my mom and the beach of "Hawaii" been beautiful.

I also send postcards to my friends and my dad and brother and we also called my dad and sees how he was doing.

The day that we would leave Hawaii, a storm was coming. But we left and we were safe but at first the plane was shaking and scaring, but it we were safe and we were safe landed in Chicago and boarded a second flight to Hartford, that day was on Palm Sunday and but we didn't go to mass, and we when to terminal and gate of the flight and about half hour later, we boarded the plane, and then about ten minutes later the plane were on the runway and soon we will be up in the air, but when it was going up it was shaking and it was a really scaring. When the plane level up it was shaking and moves back and forward and other passenger was making fun of me.

This flight from Chicago to Hartford was so bad that my mom had to hold me I was frighten and terrify, and it was the worst flight that I never took.

After I came home with my mom I went back to Jon and I had a good flight and I was not scares.

Once again, Jon was waiting for me and then we got my suitcase and walk to the car and he told that he will have an interview in San Diego and he asked if I wanted to go with him and I said yes.

Jon said maybe we will be taking the train but Jon changed his mind and Jeff took his car and we drove to San Diego and then I saw the Pacific Ocean and then we had lunch at the malls in San Diego.

We stay there for couple hours and then we headed back to LA.

On the ways back we got lost and we when by Walt DINSEY world, but so far our relationship was good but I felt that Jon was changing, but I didn't know but he did asked me to marry me. And I said yes, and I was happy and we planed to have a September wedding at the Beverly Hills Hotel and we booked. One day I told Jon that I wants to go to the Beverly center to looked for a dress and shoes, well I did looked at dress and then I notice that there was a books signing event and it was the president wife Betty Ford, at first said maybe than I said ok I will purchase the book and I did.

Then "Betty Ford" signed for me and I was happy and went I got home to Jon and I shown it too he and it said to Jean warmth and best wishes, and that was very nice. Jon came to pick me up and we had dinner at Beverly center and we also went to UCLA ands when to the library and he study and I tried to write a story and the next day we went to Kmart and I shop around and bought shoes and than we when to the farmer market and we got coffee to go and it was a good day, and than we got home and the phone rang and he took into the bathroom and I didn't know who he was talking too.

Than I knew that things were changing, but I didn't wanted to let go.

But that year I also when to Las Vega and Hawaii with my mom and I was not much with Jon and Jon was going to parties and meeting new peoples and leaving me out. But we also when to Westwood to the movie and had a lot pizzas and sizzle restaurant, but never finish was I order but Jon did.

Also Jon joins the gym so did I but I stop going and we took walks in the park and it was fun.

Now our wedding plans were on hold and cancel, and he said well let wait until I get a job and I said ok. But I was still working at the TV station but Jon and I were not getting along that good and so I somehow I find out that he was seeing Norma, and I was upset and then he told me that the wedding is off and I cried and plead with him and than I was very angry and I said how could you cheat on me? But he didn't says anything too me. Now I knew it was time for me too leave and so I pack and I when back to Connecticut and then somehow I got nervous and had a panic attack and I was not able to go outside for couples month and so it was really hard for me so, and than Jon dad died in the hospital heart attack and so there was a funeral and Jon came and told me that he got married to Norma.

They had the wedding where Jon and I would have it.

But we talk for a while and I did give him a hug and his mom Alice.

Later those days we went home and I said goodbye to Jeff and I didn't hears from him again. That was the end of Jeff and Jean love and friendship.

But I need to go back to 1985 when I came to Connecticut to visit my family and storm Gloria and I was stuck for awhile with my family but I was happy to be there at that time, and in 1986 my dad was about 64 and half and he retired from work and he got a part time job at Sears, and also J.C Penney, but he decided to keep the sears job and he was happy.

Later that time I also went me on disability and I had no choice.

At this time I was home and I was hanging with Barbie and we when to Halloween Party, Gary Craig party in Hartford and we got dress up and I was a devil woman and Barbie was a zombie.

But that was fun and we stay out late and at that time I didn't have a boyfriend. So Barbie I went out to dinner and she had a dog name sandy.

But I had a dog name Fritz, and then Barbie pick me up and pick up her friend Larry, at Kentucky fries chicken. And gave her flowers, and then they kissed and she drove him home and then we left him.

Also I took a limo one time to playhouse in New York City to that school but I was not qualified to attend. So I didn't give up on that career, but my parents were against me leaving home again, so I stay home.

I need to back about my Hawaii trip what kind of tour I took and it was Pearl Harbor and then the Arizona that sank during the war, so it was a short trip and it was nice, and then a Lau, and eating the pig and the feast and the dancer.

Also walks through the cemetery in Hawaii where the soldiers are buried.

After that we when to the pineapple factory and had delicious pineapples ice cream and I will never forget that.

I did attend Tunxis and I stay about one year and I drop out and I didn't go back because the professor thought I was not smart enough but stupid.

About one year later I drop out of Tunxis and I didn't feel that I was right for me and my I thought it was the best at that moment.

Ands my favorite radio tic 96.5 I always listen and to Gary Craig. At that time he they were located in Hartford, CT.

One day I had a bad cold and my brother when to a party and I had a cold so I told aspirin every four hours and I was watching Friday the 13th and then suddenly I started to sneeze and than I got a bloody nose and my parents tried to stop it but they couldn't stop so my dad called 911 and the ambulance arrival and they took me into the ambulance to the hospital.

After that I got release and I had to go home and had made an appointment with my nose doctor and I was fine.

I when to his office and he check out my nose and ever since that incident didn't happened again, about one month or two month my mom had chest pain and she had to go emergency room, and they monitor her head and gave her stress test like the treadmill, and then her doctor gave my mom new medicines and release her from the hospital and my dad and I when tom pick her up, before that time I called the hospital and they couldn't find my mother and I really got worry and than they find her and I was happy.

Also our neighbor said she was her daughter and they her in and her name was Chris and she was a polish neighbor and my mom took care of her children and spend time together.

One day went my mom and sister was planning to take my nephew to the bazaar they wanted to come swimming and my mom and dad said not today and they were somehow pushing peoples, ands thought they know it, but we said no and they didn't like it not at alls!

But my friend Don came over and we went to Stanley quarter park and we had some beer and then I ended up at his house and we talk and he tried to make a passed toward me and I said no, and than he took me home and my sister and my nephew were mover, and my nephew like watching

Jaws and playing on the bed in the grandparents room, and then watching a lot movie and like Rudy the red nose reindeer. Over and over, and my Nephew like that movie a lot that why he watched it was a good movie, and he was young and was very happy to watched the movie.

Well that time my dad and I own an Oldsmobile 1988 and it was a good car.

I driven it a lot and my dad too.

But also a problem car with the air condition and at that time I was thinking about going to Central Connecticut for the summer course and I thinking about it and it was like 1989 and it was it was not the right time to take it this year and I decided to take it next year but not sure at this moment of time.

Because I didn't have the money and my parents were not too thrill about me getting ahead and I just somehow listen to them.

Also my sister and my mom think that I was not smart enough and but I knew that I was so, later time I receive a catalog and I apply for Central.

Ands I was really excited about going to school soon it was going to be 1990 and it was thanksgiving and we when to my sister house and then Christmas eve and then Christmas at my sister house with the in law and I was not that thrill and so I still when and I was not that happy about it and so it was a nice time and I really didn't like the roast beef but I ate the vegetable and potatoes and it was a enough and then we when home and our dog was waited for us and the dog name was Jeff.

The dog came to the door and then he jump and we gave him the bone and then he lied down and we when to watched TV and at that time we had cable.

There was a time that we left the dog home and my sister and brother to watch the dog. But they couldn't find the dog (Jeff) but then they looked in my parent's bedroom and that where he lies on the floor and they gave him some water and some foods and they left and when we came back from New London beach the dog was waiting for us.

Then my dad took himself and then he's came inside and sat in the den room and we watched TV.

That time we had VCR and we watched the tenth command and it was a good movie and one day, we had a camcorder and my brother tape me and my dad dancing the polka and it was good and I still have that tape still.

I also tried to be a screenwriter and I send it too some Hollywood screenwriter and I also had to paid some money and they put into a catalog and but they didn't like the story so I never heard from a producer.

I also wrote songs and I send to Hilltop record and you also had to pays them and when your songs got published you would get some royalty.

But there was a few times that I did but then nothing. I also wrote poetry and got published and once again you had too pays for it.

But when time went by and I just stop doing that, and I just didn't do anything. So I just gave up on my dream.

Then my mom cousin came Sophie from New Jersey and her son and three daughter came and we had weaver chicken and then Helen Baron was over our head with her husband, and we had dinner and my mom cousin bought a watched and some jewelry that she purchase and then we when to my sister house on Valley drive and then she met my sister ands saws her godchild and then we stay for a while and the next day we when dancing at the joker wild and we went to sleep Helen and Terry and Sophie and that was the last time that we saw them but Sophie her cousin called and said I will sees you soon but I am going a tough time with my husband and then about couple month my mom called and no more Sophie and her family and they didn't live there anymore and so we tried again but there was Spanish woman answer and said no Sophie and Terry and my mom apology and hung up the phone and because my wanted to talk to her but couldn't reach her.

But my mom said why don't we tried again and once again that woman answer and we said sorry and ever since that time we didn't calls again but I have written letter and no reply has they vanish from the earth, and that was end of our cousin and but now we are not searching for them anymore. Also President Ronald Reagan visit New Britain and we when to sees him but it was a crowd and we when through security and we didn't sees him not at alls but my godmother did sees him.

End of having relatives that were close but gone forever end of 1989.

New Year 1990's

Now it is 1990 and we had happy new year together my mom and my dad and my brother and I, and we had some shrimp and potatoes chips and even pizza, so we also have champagne and we wish each other and gave kissed and it was a "Happy New Year" and then I was still alone without a boyfriend and I was lonely and depressant and I was not happy and I was stuck at home and I felt that I didn't have no freedom just being home so I decided to go to school and I tried to take some courses at Central Connecticut State University, so I took public speaking and than I took acting 101 and I took also theatre, and it was the summer program and I really enjoy doing theatre and dressing up for the part but I had a small part and I was in the mouse that roar and comedy error, and both plays I was doing a small part and trying to remember my lines some of classmate help me out and I didn't mess up with the lines and after we did the plays we had a party and we when to Steve house and we had beer and chips and it was a lot fun, and about one month later Barbie wanted to meet me for dinner but I had class so at that time she was seeing David Tem, and she wanted me to meet him, but one day I got a wrong number and I met that person that was really stupid it could been a serial killer but I didn't go inside his car and I said no way sorry it will not work, about six month later I met David because Barbie L gave me his phone number and I called him and he drove up to my driveway and we when to a strip club and then we when to Papa Gino and I had a piece of Pizza and soda and he started to talk about a business but at that time I didn't know what it was and he told me that he were take me to the meeting and it was in the day inn in Meriden, CT and I said sure I will go and I did and I found out it was Amway and so I when too a lot of meeting with him and then he became

21

my boyfriend and he didn't treated me well so. But I make time to come up stuff that he were be with me but he like to hang out in New Haven with a friend Howard. A lot times that my dad drove me to Meriden Square to wait for David and he came to pick me up and took me to the meeting every Thursday and we went to New Jersey, and then I join and I got the kit and I now I need to find customer to get some income but I was not that good and I just find peoples and pretend that they wanted to meet so I then I quit when it was not for me.

Then I met Jim and Steve and his wife and at this time Jim was single and I thought he could be more than a friend, at that I was not having good luck with men, it was going to get worse, one day I decided to called David and a lady answer the phone and I said who are you? And she said her name was Judy and she said to me I am David girlfriend and than I said that I was and then she it was getting stranger and stranger and she told me how they met.

Then I started to talk with her and she lives in New Haven and David work has a security guard at the Bella vista apartment and a lot times, David slept with a German shepherd and then his boss taught him and he got let go.

Well I was surprise when I got the phone bills and it was too high and that would help me but she was a liar. so I met her one night at the Bella Vista and also hang out and I really didn't like being there. So I thought to myself it is time to called a old friend and his name is Ricky and he live in Windsor and so I thought if David seeing that girl and his mind was only on her and so I will focus on Ricky, so I called him and make plans to sees him and at moment I felt that I was alone and I didn't have anyone and then Rick C and I decided to go to Cape cod and I thought wow! I probably will have a great time but I didn't because I felt that I pays for the gas the foods and then room that I some how empty the bank account for this trip and at that time I didn't have a cell phone so I had to call collect. And that was very expensive.

I think that I stay about one week with Ricky and one night Ricky. called ,me into the other room and said I saw a UFO and I looked I thought the same, then we had a some champagne and we cheer with each other and we had domino pizza and then I somehow vomit and then after that I fell a sleep and Ricky said I wanted to make love but you fell asleep and then we when to a different place and it was also a lot of money and I paid for everything and then we on our ways we stop at a restaurant and once again I had to paid the bills and then we headed home and about three hours later, we got to my house and Ricky and then he started to talk with my mom and said we had a wonder time and we had sex and my mom didn't want to hears that, and then he left and I was home and my mom and dad you probably spent a lot of money, and I said yes I did.

Time went by and now I was seeing Ricky less and he wanted some more money and I had to send him overnight and money to his house, and it was like bribery, and now I felt that I was being use.

Now it was September and it was Ricky. Birthday and we when to the movie and then it was less and less of seeing him so I decided to called him and now Rick C, said I was started to sound to serious and he wanted to speak to my mom and so I handle the phone to her and he said tell your daughter stop coming over my house and looking into the windows and calling me would you explained and so that night Ricky broke my heart and I cried a lot and I was really hurt that I been used and for money and sex and I was dump by him once again, and then David called and heard that I was crying and I told him and he said I will take you out and we will sees a movie and go for Pizza, and I said fine.

Couple days I invite for dinner and we had pork chop and cabbage and David really like that dish and he thanks my mom and left and went to New Haven and David like going to the malls, meet up with his friend Laura. Because he was looking for peoples for the Amway and ran into Dora Marie and David really like her but David still came over and than he came for Christmas Eve and so after that David really change and Marie was her fault and she lies to him about me saying that Jim was gay and I never said that but she did and than she said to David that Jim was hitting on her and but she kept on lying and David was believe her, and she was causing trouble.

David and I were not the same anymore and then Marie and David move to Portland and didn't give me there phone number.

One day Marie shown the gun that she had in the car and also was a witness to a bank robbery and the FBI were questionnaire her.

Then David was doing some kind of work for her and it was hush and hush and it was top secret and one day I was driving and I when there to meet up for a meeting and David push me on the sidewalks and lucky I didn't get hurt and that was still at his place in Meriden and his neighbor looked, and they drove off and I had go on a little highway to get back home and alls the ways home I cried and a lot time that David used my car and also had sex with me.

One time I decided to make home made pizza and I bought to his place but Marie said we don't have to eat now but later but David put on the oven and about twenty minute later we were eating my homemade pizza and than went outside and somehow I felt from the step on the grass, but I did not sprain my ankle and I was able to drive home but there was an other incident and that he had a driveways and he refuse to back up the car for me and I ran into the fence and I damage the car and I was very upset went I was driving home but my dad didn't yell but they were mad at "David" and ever since that time, and he move to Portland and his girlfriend pick me up and took me to the meeting and some place to eat but you could tell that she was a double cross and that were stab you in the back and then they got married and it was a secret wedding and I was not invited because didn't want me there and she thought that I would spoil the wedding but she was wrong and I was left out and my friend Jim told me because it were been much easier but I was still hurt and I didn't like how they were treating „me especially that Marie person that was probably married and use David to do dirty works for her.

With no question because he was madly in love with her and she was pregnant with his baby. So that why they got married and went she came with the baby she said she gave the baby some whisky and it sleep better.

Also her child had a hearing problem especially on the fourth of July.

Those days they came over to say goodbye because they were leaving Connecticut, and David and Marie and the Baby.

That was the last time that I saw them, again.

In those year my mom and Hilary and Sophie when to the casino together and we took the bus at the Farmington Ct and it was close to our home so Sophie pick up Helen and then us and then we took the early bus and we plays the slot machine and ate the foods in the buffet.

About two month later, Barbie and Ed when with my mom and I and Sophie and I believe that was the first time that Barbie when there.

So we stay together and Barbie and Ed then Barbie wanted to go on a ride and Ed and Barbie left for a while and she said it was not too bad.

It was time to go back to bus terminal and so us when there and waited for the bus to arrival and then we got on the bus and we headed on home.

When we arrival to Farmington Barbie and Ed were off the bus and didn't asked if we needed a ride, and we needed to called my dad and Helen never asked if we needed a money to called my dad.

So Sophie left and now we are waiting for my dad to comes and then he came and we alls got inside the car and then my dad drove home and then took Helen first home and then our home and alls the ways Helen was talking about to my dad that she never win at the casino.

Ands my dad listen to her and he couldn't wait for her to leave the car.

When we arrival home and we told my dad what kind of day that we had and it was a good day and I won a jackpot of $500.00 dollars and I was very happy and I share with my mom and dad and the rest in the bank. Later that day I called Barbie and sees what she was doing but she was busy and she was planning a wedding to Ed and she said her sister were be her maid of honor and I said that fine, but at that time I met Ed once again and I said you the guy that when to the casino you were her friend, and he nodded his head and so Barbie said you are invited to my wedding at that time I was going on a lot of trips and I was unable to attended.

About two weeks later I saw Barbie and Ed has husband and wife and went to dinner and I was very happy about my friend got married.

Couple times my dad and I went to the casino and he gave me money to gambling and it was a lot fun and he really like the breakfast buffet.

So my dad park the car at the bus station and took the bus to Foxwoods and it was a lot of fun and my dad I did a lot of things together has like going to the casino and going foods shopping and even J.C Penney shopping for clothes and shoes and for Christmas too.

I was happy when my dad stops smoking and it was good for his health.

Now they started to talk about 2000 but it was nearing 1999 and at that time I thought I was going paranoid because I order extra medicine and then make sure that we had a lot can foods and water and at that time I order a camcorder and I was thinking if it were work and at that moment I was worry and then I was really scare and we had a enough supplies and now it was Thanksgivings of 1999 and of course we were at my sister house and it was nice and than it was Christmas eve and my mom make her pirgoris and cabbage soup and pickle herring and rye bread and BABKA and it was a good holiday and then we handed out the gifts and said we will sees you tomorrow and then we when to my sister house for Christmas and she make was roast beef and mash potatoes and vegetable.

But meanwhile I am still Barbie and Ed friend and I still keep in touch with my friend Jim that use to live in Wallingford and then he move back to New Jersey and then he got married and every birthday and holiday he called me and said Happy birthday and he is a good friend.

About a week later it was New year Eve and the whole family were together my mom and dad and I were celebrating New Year eve in the living room with shrimp and champagne and we would waiting for the ball to drop and then but the music was playing Dick Clark on New Year Eve on ABC about 1130 pm, and soon it will be that new year and that year I had money trouble and I tried not to filed anything in the court, but I was harassment by the creditor and I had no choice at that time to file bankrupt. My lawyer was very nice and said you will receive more offer to get a credit card and in 10 year it will be fine and so I had no choice I did file and that was done, and I did have too have separate account and I couldn't have joint account at that point and that was the day at the court and then soon the ball will fall and my dad was ready to stay cheer and so was I and my mom and my brother and we were together, and then my dad got up and hit my glass and my mom and my brother and in few second it was going to be 2000 and a new year.

At that moment I was really scare and I didn't says much but still it was 1999. And then it was 2000 and my dad said hope that you live and have happy lives and we said the same and my dad kissed my mom and me and gave my brother shook hands and it was a new year. Then my mom friends passed away Hilary and Sophie and then we were going less to the casino.

$2\cancel{0}\cancel{0}\cancel{0}$'s

It was 2000 and that day were going to have leg of lamb and that for lunch and that was my father favorite foods and mint jelly and we had that and couples day later I got my first computer and it was a gateway. From 1995 to 2000 I didn't have a boyfriend and I was alone, so I decided to put ads in AOL to find a man that I could have and love and not being lonely.

But I didn't exactly meet this man but his Name is Joey and we started to Instant message on AOL and then he emails me and then us sometime we talk on the phone. And he was very nice and then I was talking to someone else like his name was Bruce and he was from Berlin and seem like he was friendly but I did meet him and he took me to Friendly in Newington and it was nice but we didn't hit it off and then there was Steve from Norwich but we stay about three hour in "Town and Country Pizza" and he gave me flowers and we had a good times but he just wanted to be friends. And I was too happy about that. Then I met a Sal also at the pizza place but he was seeing a Spanish lady and said sorry and then I met a man Chunk and he looked at me and said no it is not going too work, thought that I was not the type that he was looking for and also my teeth were not prefect with a tooth missing.

But now I knew I had a problem and I needed to fix my teeth and they were out and bad and but before that one man suppose me too meet me at the pizza place and drove away in his green JETTA and I didn't hear from his again and more men just took off and it was really painfully and there was one incident that man name Tom came to pick me up too take me to the movie and but then he said he had a headache and drove me home, and that was the end of that too. Then I was driving the Subaru to the Marriott Hotel in Farmington, to meet men, but each one wanted sex and so I said no and then there was a man from Waterbury and he tried to convince to go to his hotel room and got me a drink and I said no and then there was a other man that make a pass in the parking lot and I didn't see that person again and there was one more that got me dinner and tried to take me into the woods and have sex with him and I said no but he tried to rape me and I felt dirty, because I was assault by him, and when I got home I wash myself and bad about myself, and then time when by and there was a nice man and he send me his photo and I said no-way I am going to meet him because he was not handsome but then I thought to myself well maybe I will sees him and if I don't like him I will not sees him again, so his name was Gary J. Stagliano and he was very nice and bald and I met him on September 7, 2001 at town and country pizza and he drove into the parking lot of WALMART and got out of the car and he came toward me and asked " are you Jean Marie" and I said yes and we when inside and sat down at the booth and we order a pizza and we talked and he took about his ex wife (Ann) and about his divorce and I listen and then he gave me a gift and it was a little box and necklace and it was very nice and I agree to sees him that night to sees a movie at Lowe theatre in Plainville, but at that time I was not sure if I really wanted to sees him but I did that night and after the movie we walks and talks in the parking to early morning, Gary and I enjoy going to the movies.

Gary told me that he own a hobby shop in Manchester Ct, on west middle turnpike and he said I would like you too see it and I also want to meet your parents but it didn't happened, so it took like couples month before I introduce Gary to my parents. Also Gary Told me that has a son and daughter, and there names are Nickolas and Catherine, and I said that is nice.

So Gary and I when to Friendly and Applebee for dinner and so time when by and I introduce Gary to my parents about 4 month later, at that time I was not sure that my parents like him or not, but Gary gave his business card to my parents and Gary said you have no reason to worry about Jean, because she will be safe with me, and my parents shook there heads.

Then one day I told Barbie about Gary and asked her if she could take me to Manchester and she said if we go to Boston Market and also I need money for Gas and Barbie said I want $20.00 dollars for gas and I said ok.

First we when to Boston Market and I order the chicken but I didn't eat much and then Barbie took me to Gary and parked the car and Barbie came inside to Meet Gary and then I introduce and Barbie said nice too meet you and Gary said the same and then, Barbie left me and I called my mom and said I am ok and that was the first night that I stay with Gary. And my parents was ok with that's. it was time to meet his children Nickolas and Catherine and Gary wanted me to go with him to pick the children but at first I was not going and he asked my mom and my mom said ok and Gary said don't worry mama, Jean Marie will be fine, so Gary came to pick me up and it was time to meet his children and I was not sure how they were react and we were going to there aunt house to pick them up and not to the ex wife but his ex wife packed whole lot and so Gary and I pack the van and the children climb inside and they went into the back and then Gary backed up the van and than we were headed to back to Connecticut, and that night I was going to stay with Gary and the children at the west middle turnpike and it was near the store, Father and sons hobby shop.

Like I was saying the holiday were coming and it was going to be thanksgivings and I did decided to stay with Gary and his children and my mom and dad when to my sister house, if it was different Gary and I and the children were been included but we were not.

It was one day before thanksgiving and Gary bought a chicken and stuff and vegetable and so we were going to have our first thanksgiving together.

This is my story how I met Gary it was September 7, 2001, when I met Gary Joe, I met Gary over the internet and he send his photo and I like it and I sent my photo to Gary. He looks at my picture and I said I would meet him for lunch, and I said yes. I accept his invitation for lunch and we went to town and country pizza for lunch. After lunch I walk him to his car, and then Gary gave me a kiss, and then he asked me if I wanted to see a movie and I said yes to Gary. I met him at the movie and after the movie I stay out late with Gary. It was after midnight and I didn't want to leaves him, that night.

The next morning Gary called me and asked if I want meet him at friendly in west Hartford and I said I will meet you, but before I went too see him I went Barbie house and asked if she could shown how to gets there so I follow her and we ended up at Elmwood and not the right friendly.

I waited and waited and he didn't show up I thought he stood me up but later went I got home I receives a lot messages from Gary and he was very worried about me and I explains I went to the wrong location, and he was fine.

Gary asked me if I wanted to see a movie and I said yes again and I met Gary again at 7pm the next day.

At that time I was really getting exciting to see Gary again; I knew that Gary felt the same about me.

After the movie we walk around and find bleacher and sat there for a wile and went home afterward, but I didn't wants to leaves.

But Gary asked me went will I meet your parents but not yet! But time when by and he did meet my parents and my mom make coffee and cake and Gary said nice too meet you and shook my dad hands and gave my mom a hug and they talked for while and Gary left and said I will sees you tomorrow and he gave me a kissed and hug.

When Gary left my mom and dad said we really like Gary and he is a very nice man and friendly, and I agree with them and at time I planned to sees Gary mores.

When Gary got home he gave me a called and I was happy to talk with and then he said Goodnight to me and he hung up the phone.

The next day Gary called and said good morning and how are you doing and I said fine and then he said to me I will have my breakfast and then I will open store and I will talk with you later, and I said ok and bye.

Then Gary called me up and asked if I had plan for tonight and I said no and said do you want to go to the movie and I said yes, and I will be at your house at 7pm and I said I will see you later.

Later that day and I saw Gary coming in the white van toward my house down the hill and Gary turn into my driveway and got out car and rang the doorbell and I said mom and dad I will see you later and I said bye and I close the door and went to the van and went inside Gary gave me a kissed and hold my hand all the ways to the house and then we got to the theatre and then Gary Purchases the tickets and then Gary got popcorn and cherry soda and we share it, when we were watching the movie and after the movie Gary took me to "Applebee" and then Gary took me home and came inside for a while and left home and gave me a kiss, once again.

When he arrive at home Gary gave me a called and said I am home and I will talk with you tomorrow, and Gary said I have to do store things right now and I said bye and I said ok.

The holiday were coming and Gary asked am I coming invite for the holiday and I said of course you are, but later I found out that for thanksgiving and Gary said well I will have the thanksgiving with my children and I said so will and I am not going to my sister house if I am not welcome and you were not included not because my sister didn't want to comes over but she was worry about the in law would asked a lot of questions, so Gary and I and the children had our own Thanksgiving and Gary bought a chicken and I make the stuffing and I heated up the gravy and we had green bean and we celebrate the thanksgiving has a family.

In someway Gary was a bit upset that he was not included and his children and then it he was fine.

Even on thanksgiving Gary when to the store and said I will not be long so you take care of Nickolas and Catherine so I did, and then when Gary was finish at the store he put on a DVD and we watched it, and then it was bedtime and before I went to sleep I called my parents to says that everything is ok and I asked how they were doing and they were fine.

On thanksgiving week I stay with Gary and then we drove the children back to his ex wife Ann, but we before we left we stop at my house for a pit stop and my mom was ok with that and we were headed to Pennsylvania, to Stroudsburg and the Children were in the back of the van and I was in the front with Gary and I check on them once in a while and on the ways there we stop at Mc Donald for lunch and after lunch we continue and then the next stop Gary took a nap so did Nickolas and Catherine and I sat and looked at them, and then they woke up and we were on our ways there.

Then Gary put on the rock and rolls station and starting to sing and the children would take a nap at that moment.

We would on 84 headed toward Danbury to reach 209 toward strouburg and Gary drove and drove and then he was saying that he was getting tired and need to rest.

Also Gary said that he felt bit down because he had to leave his children with his ex wife.

Went we got there his ex wife Gary and me some onion soup and Gary accepts and I said no thank you to Ann.

Also Gary took some on the road then said that he got some heartburn, after eating the soup. Then Gary asked if I was hungry, I said I was and we stop at Wendy, and I got chicken nugget that day for dinner.

After that stop, we would head to Connecticut and I couldn't wait to gets home and being alone with Gary.

Before we got home we took a rest stop and took a little walk and I also called my mom and told now we are heading home.

About a month later, it was going to be Christmas, so once again, but she bought the children on Christmas day but on Christmas eve, Gary came over my house and that night he met my sister and brother in law and aunt Heather, and Gary spoke about his hobby shop to them, and Aunt Heather I will bring in a game to your store and Jeanne will show me where.

After the dinner they kept on talking and then my sister and her family left and Gary was still here and we watched a movie, and then he when home too and he gave me a kiss and a hug, at that time we had a dog name Alex.

Time when by and Gary asked me to move in so I spend my weekend with Gary and so my dad and brother took me to Manchester and I spent a lot of time with Gary, and his children.

Then Gary told me about his campaign about his D&D game and then I join them and I when over and played them too.

The game was like every Saturday night and we had to pick character and play the game.

Then his friend Bill had an other D&D and I also join that group too but Bill was a Wicca, but he was a nice person to know, and those game would great too play with them.

But then Gary asked me if I wanted to go with him to the convention and I did go with him and I was his cashier and I sold a few games, and he was proud of me and sometime I was alone in the store and I was in charge.

When Gary had to the bank I watched the store and some customers came in and I sold like Buffy card and games and much more, and Gary asked how did I do and I said well and Gary also gave me a working for him a pays and I said you don't have too but he did.

Then I met Cheryl and then I met Carl, Greg, David, but I felt that David didn't like me.

After we played Gary took me to dinner to Shady Glen and we share a hot fudge sundae, and then we walks in the parking lot of stop and shop to have some exercise and Gary was holding my hand and holding me close.

Than we stop at Dunkin Donut for coffee and a donut that was every Sunday with Gary, but Gary most of the time Gary had a coffee and a bagel, and then we watched a movie that night too.

On Tuesday night, Gary had Anime Night and I met his friend Chris and also I met Ryan and some guy from West Hartford that Gary picks up once in awhile. We watched a few amines and then Gary make popcorn and one time he almost started a fire in the kitchen and but he was ok.

After we ate the popcorn, and then Gary fell asleep and started to snore and Chris was laughing and then when Gary woke up Chris started to tease Gary.

Gary said to Chris that he was not sleeping but Chris said yes you did, and back and forward. After the anime was finish everyone left and then Gary close the door behind them and lock the door and shut off the lights and then we when to bed. It was about 3 am I woke up and I looked and Gary was not in the back so I got up and Gary was walking and talking in his sleep and so he was sleeping walking and I did wake him and Gary and he said what am I doing here? Then he when back to sleep, and woke up a lot and I follow him and he was a sleep.

But there was a lot time that Gary awoke up and woke me up and said I had a bad dream and told me about it and then he when back to sleep, and also Gary told me bedtime stories and then he called me a polish princess.

The next morning Gary make the coffee and a bagel and then we had breakfast and he called his mom and dad and then we when into the hobby shop to open and sometime I was there alone and Gary did his computer work and then he came inside the store and then price items and then sometime on Monday we went to the warehouse to picks up games and model cars and for the hobby shop.

Sometime the warehouse didn't have that in stock so Gary orders it and so I help Gary out a lot.

Sometime Gary took a lot time in the bathroom, I was in bed waiting for Gary to comes and so put my head on the pillow and then Gary came and I Gary started to talked and then suddenly he started to speak gibbering to me and then he fell asleep and then few minute later I heard sound and I thought he was speaking to me and I was really scare that night.

Almost every night I heard some kind of noises and when I was vacuuming the rug and I thought it was Gary but there was no one there. So, I left the apartment and I went into the store and stay with Gary and I also make lunch and sometime dinner and a lot time Gary and I when to Outback and it was fun and one time that Ed and Barbie came over and we when to the outback and we when into Barbie car and after dinner we when back to Gary place and Barbie and Ed left and we when inside and Gary close the door and we got change and we when to bed and the next morning was Sunday and Gary and I when to church to saint Bridget, and Gary took the van and drove there and then after the mass we when there for breakfast.

About noon Gary friends came over and they plays game likes Axis battle games and sometime I played too. Sometime I took a walks and when to Pepe Pizza on west middle turnpike and had lunch there alone and sometime I bought something for Gary too.

Later that day Gary drove me home and Gary stays for awhile and then left and when he got home he called me. I talked with Gary awhile and I was very happy to hear his voice.

One day Gary told me and the children that we were going to Saint Bridget to the bazaar and Nickolas and Catherine were excited about it so we walks up west middle turnpike and the children were in front of us and we watched them and then we got to the bazaar and we walk inside the parking lot and Gary told me to take the children to the picnic table and to wait for Him to bring the foods for us and for himself, so Gary bought got for us was hot dogs and fries and sodas. And after we ate we started to walks around and then Gary asked Nickolas if he wanted to go on the ride and Nickolas said yes and Catherine refuse and hold on to her dad.

So Nickolas took off his shoes and climb that ride and then slide down and Gary said do you want to do it again and Nick said yes, and once again he did and meanwhile, Catherine watched, then Catherine decided to go on the ride but Gary said it is time to go home and then Catherine started to cried and I try to conform her but she refuse and started to cried.

But then she stop at one spot and she said I want to do this and she got a fishing rod and then a prize and she was really disappoint about the prize and then she started to cried and screamed alls the ways home and Gary said, stop crying Catherine, everyone is looking at us and she said so what!

When we got home Catherine storm inside and started to scream and yelled and then the phone rang and it was Gary ex wife Ann, and Gary spoke to Ann and then the ex wanted to speak to Catherine but at first she refuse to speak to her mom, but Catherine was still angry at Gary and me.

After Catherine spoke to her mom but she still refuse to go to bed so she snuck into Gary and my bed and refuse to leave and then Gary took Catherine to her bedroom and told her a bedtime story and sometime I did too.

About 3 am Catherine was in bed with me and Gary and Gary was fast asleep and the next morning Nickolas jump in and said is Jean Marie will be my new step mother and at that moment Gary and I didn't know what to says to Nickolas. Later that day I make coffee and I make toasted bagel for Gary, and Nickolas, and Catherine and I didn't have that's!

After breakfast we when next door to the hobby shop and Catherine and I played together and then, at lunch time Catherine when next door to Vic Pizza for lunch and Gary and Nickolas had lunch later that day and also Catherine and I when for a walks down the stairs and I always hold her hand and when we cross the street and even walking down the hills and there one time that Catherine wants kind of ran down the hill and I said wait for me and she did.

Then Catherine I went to the park for awhile and then we headed back to store to see her dad and my boyfriend Gary, went we got back they would playing chess, and Nick was winning.

Then Gary gave a kiss and a hug and Catherine and sat at the table for awhile and then Gary close the store about 2pm and we all took a nap.

Later that day I make dinner and then wash the dishes and went next door to the hobby shop and help out Gary.

Every time I went with Gary to take the children back to Ann and pick them up but there was a snow storm and Gary went by himself.

There was a time that I was with Gary and he came up to me and show me his wedding ring and he got me off guard and I didn't know what to says to him and then he put the rings away and said I show you the ring again and then after it didn't happened again! I think that Gary was asking me to married him and I was just like in shock.

I was speechless and I couldn't understand why? Then there was a time that Gary and I stay home and dance in the living room and sometime when it was hot in the bedroom we slept in the living room floor with sleeping bags and cuddle with each other and Gary hold me all night long and I hold Gary tight.

In the summer when Nickolas and Catherine , and Gary and I took the walks around the block and stop at the park and the children plays and then we stop at Vic sometime for dinner and sometime I make dinner.

About one month later Gary join the barter club and they were having a party and Gary and I when and there were a lot of peoples there and Gary bought me a glass of coke and rum and Gary had the same drink has I did, and there was music and we danced. And then we left and when home and Gary stop by the store and pick up his phone and we when inside.

Then we when to sleep and the next morning we overslept for church and afternoon Gary friends came over and they played a zombie game and a lot I didn't win but almost of the time Gary won.

But with Gary we when to convention to Stratford and then we when to a other one in Pennsylvania and then we pick up Nickolas and Catherine and the time that I thought I lost Nickolas in a Mc Donald restaurant and we find him at the plays room and Gary was a bit mad at me but I stay with Catherine and it was fine and Gary order the food and we ate it and we headed to the car and headed to Connecticut.

Once in the while I looked in back and see what the children were doing but they were taking a nap in the back.

There was one summer that Gary came with the children and they were sweating and Gary asked if they could go swimming I think that day I said no because of my mom. But Gary and the children came for picnic and we had hot dogs and hamburger and one time Gary got overstuff and didn't feel good and so he said I think I want to go home and Gary did.

When the holiday came Gary was welcome and it was Thanksgivings and Catherine said daddy you are sleeping at the table wake up and then Nickolas knife was falling off the table and once again Catherine, said what are you going Nick? But he didn't say anything, but I was sitting quiet.

My mom and dad and my brother also sat at the dinning room table and it was a happy time and I remember it very much, and how happy I was.

But that year that Gary didn't come was Christmas eve because Ann bought the children on the day of Christmas eve and Gary was didn't comes because his ex wife stay overnight and then the storm came in and so that year I didn't see Gary, but the year before Gary and I spend New year eve and we first when to the restaurant and the salad was like in a hot dish and it should been in a cold dish and the waitress was rude and I don't remember if Gary gave her a tip.

After we left the restaurant and we were headed to Connecticut and then I called my mom and said I am fine and I said "Happy New Year" and then we got to Gary and mine place and then we talked and then Gary said I will give you a bath and then Gary put on the water and then the water was ready for me and then I went into the bathtub and then Gary wash me and then he join me and we kissed and after the bath Gary carry me to the bed in my towel and wipe me.

Then Gary laid next me and holds me tight. And he hold me all night long, and the next morning I make the coffee and took my iron pill and called my mom and later that day, Gary and I went to house for New year dinner and then Gary stay for awhile and then left.

Before Gary left, Gary gave me a kissed and I walk Gary to the car and I watched Gary backup his car and left and then went he arrival home and Gary gave me a called and then I spoke to Gary awhile.

I felt some of his friends didn't like me very much and but Gary didn't care because he loved me and I loved him and nothing else didn't matter.

So let me tell you about the time that we when to Pennsylvania on Mother day when Gary said I spend every year with Ann and I want you to comes with me and I was not sure, but Gary said well I will get a flowers for you and my ex wife Ann and I will explained to your mom that I really wants you to comes with me and at that moment I said yes.

But first we stop at my house and said to my mom and dad I will be ok with Gary about going to Pennsylvania, and so we left and I had my cell phone and I did called my mom and there were moment that I also text my friend Joe and told him what was going on with me and Gary and there were moment that I cried that Gary got me upset and I cried and Gary said you are very emotional and I really love you.

So we arrival and we were going to sleep at the ex wife home and we slept on the sofa,, and I felt out of place so I and Gary stay in bed and then Ann was making breakfast and she was making pancakes and then she notice that she used bad eggs and she toss out that batch of pancakes and started all over again and than we when to church and then we when to subway for lunch.

I told Gary that I had an upset stomach but Ann tried to give me something I refuse to take it and then later that afternoon we watched TV.

But I knew the next morning we were going back home and so I was happy and I did call my mom and dad and sees how they were doing but they were fine.

Well we reach Waterbury and then the car broken down and I told Gary that I had triple a and so the police officer called a tow truck and we ended up at Day inn and it was a nice time and that week stay for the whole weeks with Gary at west middle turnpike, and later that day my brother and dad came to pick me up in front of Vic Pizza and I got inside the car, and we drove home, and Gary stay inside the store that day and there was another incident that my brother and dad drop me off and my dad had to used the bathroom and my dad use the one in the store, and my dad said it was terrible and awful and my dad no more I am going into that bedroom and I didn't forget what my dad said, that day.

Now I need to says that Gary told me to invite Ed and Barbie and I make my chill and Gary put into the slow cooker and added Marconi and we had salads and then we had desert and Barbie and Ed enjoyed our dinner and then that day I bought thirteen ghosts and Barbie was not too happy about that a lot time that Barbie hide her head on Ed shoulder and it was a good evening and then we stay up after 2 am and before they left I didn't want to stay alone in the apartment so I asked Barbie and Ed to stay with me until Gary came back from the store and they did and Barbie said I thought you were not scare, but that night I was.

There was time that Barbie and Ed came over to visit Gary and I and we played once zombies but Barbie was not sure at that time but Barbie did played and also played settle of cataan, and that night we really stay up long.

But Gary and I won and they lost and Barbie said you must have cheating and I said no we didn't.

After they left Gary close the door and we when to sleep and I was close to Gary and a lot time I pretend that I was sleeping but I heard when he came to bed. So the bedroom was not big but it was also not small there was a window on the left of the room and the middle and there was like a little table and the bed was in the middle and then on like the walls there was closet and then there and carpet on the floor and Gary slept on his right and I slept on my left and going out of room, you ended up in a room hallway and it was close to two bedroom that was on the left of the hallway and then a right one but that bedroom someone punch a hole in the wall, and there was a twin bed and a computer in that room that was Nickolas room and then the other room was Catherine and Catherine was afraid of her room and said there were monster and she always came into Gary and mine room when she visit her dad. So in the front of 149 west middle turnpike it was a brick building with a picture window and a white door and that would have been 147 the residence of Gary J. Stagliano, and the next door was his hobby shop and so Gary didn't to have travel far to work.

So when you were coming in the front door you enter the living room and you saw the TV and the DVD and a park bench near the window, and you saw a chess board near the window and the other side Gary had book case and a lot of books.

Then when you left the living room you enter the kitchen with and you saw a kitchen table and chair and on your left it was the kitchen with the washer and dryer and then the counter and stove and microwave and so that is the kitchen, and I have told about the bedroom and also had walls papers with cup and dishes and also locate in kitchen table was the side door, where Gary white van was parked and locked.

In Gary store he had a small room for his computer and where he work and fell asleep and he told me that I should know how to open the store in case if case of emergency and also Gary let us drive his van in a parking lot in case if he needed me to take over when we when to Pennsylvania.

But every time that I saw Gary he save me a hug and kissed and hold me tight and one it was Gary birthday my brother and I bought Gary some chicken and noodle and vegetable and Gary was very happy and then I gave him a give and I stay awhile but then I left with my brother and then I called Gary and told him that I am ok.

There was a time that Gary and I were in bed and then he started to rub my feet and then Gary notice that I had a bump and so I told my doctor and I make a appointment with Dr. Jolly and when I went to him he took x ray and said if it does not bother you and we shouldn't do the surgery.

At a later time I met Steve and Kyle from New Britain and he work for Gary and then one day I when with them to get some dinner at then I bought some home for Gary. But Gary a lot of times from Domino pizza and so Gary and I had leftover and so we really like pizza, one time I bought something from home and I gave to Gary and he forgot and it was in the microwave and so the next day it was not good.

Also my mom gave Gary some of her beef stew and also chicken soup and he share it with Bill, Chris and Ryan.

One day I went into the apartment to drink some soda and some how I started to choke and Gary came up to me and told me to relax and I would be fine and I remember when Gary got hurt and I had to help him with the his toe and then I his step had blood spot and Gary wash it off.

One day Gary and I and my mom when to Foxwoods and we when to dinner and Gary was not too happy about the buffet and then he when to the bathroom and we lost him and we when around and around looking for Gary and then we went for coffee and then he left and we order a pie and so left the restaurant and once again we looked for him and then we found him and it was time to go home. But we were worry about Gary.

Gary and I and Ryan went and I watch Ryan and sometime we switch seat and I got stuck in the back with a seatbelt or seat to sit just on the floor of the van and then we stop for awhile and then we continue to travel to get to Nick birthday party and that time Ann was seeing a new man and I don't even remember his name and so we met and we all sat at that pizza place and we had cake and then Ryan and Nickolas talk but Catherine was more talking to Ryan and then Nickolas, and it was a nice time and then after the party we when home and once again Gary was upset.

On the ways Back home I sat in front of the van and Ryan in bed and so I think that Ryan took a nap and some way home we had to stop because Ryan to go to the bathroom.

Later that night I met Karen but she had a broken elbow and Gary spoke to her and I when inside the house and Gary came in a few minute later and we when to sleep.

The next morning we were planning to go to church but we overslept and so we stay home in bed and Gary sometime told me stories and so it was a good time and sometime I told Catherine about Cow with boots and she really like that story ands said what happen next.

Gary and I went to Middlefield to the library and played with his gamers and then we had lunch and I brought buffalo chicken and mustard and we had a good lunch there and then after that we played all sorts of games and I met Cheryl and then I met Greg and other peoples and that was like every second Saturday at the library and Gary had a high school student his employee to work when we went to the library and later we when to the dinner and a movie also.

Also in the store Gary had a Tenjo games and the player would Gary and I and Jessica and her boyfriend and Jessica and her boyfriend won and then they receive the prize was a tee shirt and it was Tenjo tee shirt and I also got one because I played the game.

This game took hour and hour to finish it but Jessica and her boyfriend won and then Jessica went back to work at the counter and some customer came in.

On good Friday Gary and I and Nickolas and Catherine came to colors eggs and they really had a lot of doing and that is the tradition in the Rusin.

Also friends would David and Joe, but Joe and David came over mostly on Sunday and Gary use his kitchen has the gamers where they axis to allies.

That day Joe came over and then Liz and her husband and then we played the games, and on Saturday we had others games or role playing too. And then we had domino pizza and twice I had people choice and had it in the restaurant, but a lot I was hungry and then I decided to go on my own and sometime to the Mobil station for milk and sometime I went alone to Wendy for chicken nugget and fries. But Gary and I spend a lot of time together.

One day again we would invite to Todd and Pam house for dinner and after we ate we played the game and then we went home and we said goodbye and we left and we got home and Gary parked his van and we got out and Gary took out his house key and unlock the door and we went inside and once again Gary gave me a bath and then he join me in the bath and later he wipe me off and we make love and then we fell asleep.

On good Friday Gary and I and Nick, Catherine, we colors eggs and then we went for a walk around the block the year was 2003, and Easter was two days later, and the next day the priest would comes and bless the foods and that day we didn't eat meat until EASTER.

So my mom and I would ready for Easter and our guests would coming over about in one hour and so now had to put in the scallop potatoes and macaroni and cheese in the oven and then the kielbasas was boiling in the pot.

Soon my sister and brother in law will comes over and my two nephews Robby and Mike and then Gary and Nickolas and Catherine will comes afterward and then we will have Easter together, and it will be a good day.

But at this time I am looking out for my sister and her family and meanwhile Gary called and said right now he is giving the children breakfast and Gary said I will sees you soon and said that is great, and about ten minutes later my sister arrival and then they park the car and they came inside and Susie is not letting them sit and so we give her a bone and she lay on the corner of the dinning room and then my mom and sister cut the kielbasa and I bring in the macaroni and cheese and scallop potatoes to the dinning room table and then my dad enter and the rest of the family and then we says pray and then we eat our meal, and about one hour later, Gary arrival with the children and then I told them to follow us into the dining room and then we sat down and had our Easter dinner and then after Gary and I when up to my room because Gary wanted to rest a bit and then later we took a walk and Catherine stay with my mom and dad. Later Gary ands I and Nickolas came back and that night I went with Gary to Manchester and I was going to bring the children back to Gary ex wife on Holy Monday, and so I when over and we watched some anime and then we put the children to sleep and we both when into our bedroom and then we fell asleep.

The next morning we got up and got ready and pack the stuff for Catherine and Nickolas and we were on our ways.

Before we left we stop at my parents house and told them that we were headed to Stroudsburg Pennsylvania, and my mom always said be careful and Gary said don't worry, because I do care for your daughter and you have nothing to worry about.

After we left on the road Gary said did you pack any sandwiches? I said nope I forgot and so he said that is ok, but in 2002 we did make ham sandwiches from Easter ham. But I am sorry and Gary understood and we stop at McDonald and I got a chicken sandwich and fries and after lunch and we stop at an other rest stop where Gary and the children took a nap and I was sitting, about half hour and we were on our way, and we were headed to his ex wife home.

There was another rest stop and Catherine looked out and said why are here so many stone and Gary didn't says anything about that but he took a nap and I told Catherine it was a cemetery near the road and Catherine said what is a cemetery, I didn't know how to explained to her but I said nothing.

So we were not going to Ann house but to Ann sister house and so when we got there and she said to me Ann Marie, and Gary said this is Jean Marie, and but she didn't hear him and Gary said that he felt that he was invisible.

After we left we stop at the dollar store and Gary purchase some stuff even for me and the children and I took with me and Gary drop me off and Gary said he were called me when he got home and before I did Gary gave me a kiss and then Gary back out of the driveway and then I went inside.

About half hour later Gary Called and I talked with Gary and I said I would talk with Gary on Tuesday April 22, 2003 about 1030pm and at that time I was watching the movie the "Ring" and it was a really scaring movie and after I watched I was scare, but Gary said that Gary were would come over for Breakfast on April 23, 2003, and I said it great and I cannot wait to sees you and so that morning of the April 23, 2003 and I got up about 7am and I told my mom and dad that Gary was coming over and my mom said I will save Gary some of the hazelnut coffee and now it is about after 9 am and Gary was still not here and I called the house and I thought it was a new message, and I think I called about 1030 am and I thought Gary was running late, so I waited and called about 1100 am and still the same message and I called and asked Judy if Gary was van was in the yard, and then few minute later, she called and said probably one of his friend pick him up and I said no, he suppose to comes to my house and then I said why don't you looks through the window and she said nothing, and then I said maybe you should called the Police and said no I don't want to get in trouble about noon I called the Manchester Police and explained that my boyfriend own a hobby shop and he is not answering his phone were you find out if he is all right!

About half hour later, I receive that they found Gary in bed with a face mask and why he was wearing a mask? I said I don't know, and they were working on him and they were get back to me and about half our later they said Gary Passed away and they wanted to me to go to the morgue to looked at the body so I told them about Pam and Todd and they went to sees the body and it was Gary.

At that moment, I couldn't believe that he was gone.

So that day I called my friend Joe and I told him that Gary Passed away and I was crying a whole lot and I really couldn't speak to Joe and Joe knew that I was hurting, and I tried to listen to him, but my heart was breaking because I lost my best friend and my love and I really couldn't handle it so, I cried and I thought that maybe they were wrong and it was not Gary, but the next day I called Joe and I was still hurting and I still crying for Gary very much.

But Joe listen to me and then the next Gary landlord contacting me about things in the apartment and someway I was afraid to be in the apartment where Gary lived, but I did go and I met Gary younger brother Gino and Gary Ex wife Ann and Nickolas and Catherine were there.

That day before I ran into Gary ex I when with my brother Walter and pick up the vacuum and took it too my house and also handed the key to his landlord and left and then the second time I when there with Pam and Todd because he wanted to pick up his game and I also lost the game that I order from Gary and someone else took it and I lost my money.

Pam and Todd came inside the hobby shop and Gino introduce himself and Todd said I need to take my game but Gino said you have to wait until it goes through the court and I also cannot believe that Ann gave my bathrobe to Goodwill and she knew it was not Gary but mine.

Somehow I forgot to grab it from the closet but now it is gone.

In three day they are going to have a memorial service for Gary and I am going with Pam and Todd to the funeral home and then the next day to the church to Saint Bridget, and that day I really cried for Gary so much and I didn't sees him because he was cremated and he was just in a small container, and alls Gary Friend would there and Gino took a pictures, and the next day it was held at Saint Bridget Church and I was sitting with Ann and Catherine and Nickolas and Gino, and after the mass we alls stand out on the sidewalk and I talked with Gino and Ann and the children and then all the peoples that attended the memorial service, we when to Pepe for lunch but Ann and the children and Gino when back to Gary Place and the only interested was would the children receive benefit from social security from Gary, and then they went to court but they said that he abandon and not probate court, and then they sold his things from the store.

At that time I felt grief and loss of Gary and I still didn't believe that Gary was gone. The day of the memorial was April 29, 2003.

Also Gary went to the time machine, and his name was Steve that sometime purchase from Gary store for his store and Steve somehow gave Gary less money for products. Then I also that Joe and Gary would work on a game but they didn't complete it.

I went to crusade, Runecon, ELIIS CON, and east coast.

I just to have memories of Gary, and lifetime was our destiny to be together, but fate had other plans Gary and I so that day of his death everything change I loss my best friend that was special to me and I will never forget Gary, he will be always in my heart.

That someone precious to me I will never forget him.

Gary was friendly and kind to me and he treated me good and but there were days that he did make me cried and then he gave me a hug and kiss and hold me tight.

The story that I have told you about Gary travels from Michigan to Connecticut to build his own business, once in Connecticut the man, Gary Joe begins to make his dreams of becoming his own boss a realization.

Many of his customers enjoy stopping by and participating in games such has TENJO, Battle cry, and settler of Cataan with Gary Joe in his store.

Gary Joe always enjoys sharing his games with his customers while playing with them himself.

Why am I an Author?

Okay, I think, therefore I am. But who gets to play that game? A New Born? A mosquito? A Computer? My thoughts are here or there?

When I no longer think once did, am I think as once did am I same Person? What composes this "I, molecules, memories?

Now I begins to write my first book and the title is Father and Sons Hobby (Dreams do comes true) Gary Joe Story.

This story will take you on a true story that Gary struggles of everyday of his life until to the end. Gary Joe was able to be successful and remain sweet and kind to the end of his life.

This story will make you cried and then it might make you laughed because Gary was very important and special to me and I wanted his good memories to live on with this book, and the book got published on October 31, 2003.

Yes this book was self – published and it helped me with the loss and pain of losing Gary, because he meant a lot too me.

So I written "Father and Sons Hobby" book and then I written poetry about Gary, because I was thinking of Gary whole lot so I just was couldn't stop and so here are the poem that I written to about Gary.

The little poem book called is Memories of my love.

September 7, 2001, the day that I met Gary, that was the happiness day of my life. I would not change it not at all, we had fall for each others and it was about two year and now he is gone, but I will keep the memories forever and I will have no more tears to fall, I will keep Gary in my heart forever, I will never forget this wonderful man, he will be in my heart always!

Then I written this poem "voice of Gary I hear in my heart, every nights I dreams of Gary, I hear his voice he is calling my name, then I wake up, I don't see your face anymore, my love will be strong, you are in my heart and soul forever, and every night I will dream of you, Gary.

Happy birthday November 14, memory of your birthday Gary J. Stagliano, the day will be special but you will not have no carrot cake but I will always remember you on your special day, happy birthday Gary, I will be missing you but you are in my heart and the love that you gave me I will never forget you, I will be loving you forever my dearest friend, one day we will be together again. Happy birthday in heaven and you are in my heart forever my love. Here is more poem that I written, missing you, the day I met you, with you that make me smile on your face, when you touch me on my face, when you touch me went we would together, the day that you didn't show up, I knew that something was wrong, when you died, and now I am missing you so much. But I still have the pain but now it is less, but I miss you so much, so this year is that Gary passed away over 7 years ago and I still miss Gary because he was very special to me, always.

After I written Gary book, so I got different idea and I written my second book and it was called " No Ending Dreams" and I did gets a press release for Father and sons and then for this book, but when I got my first book I thought I was going to be on the bestseller list for the New York Times, but I thought at that time that you just published the book and you get on the list, but you don't and you need to promote yourself and then maybe your local newspaper will do an article on you if you are lucky, well yes I did gets called from the Hartford courant and then the New Britain Herald, so I got two reporter to comes over my house and they did the interview, but the courant didn't published the story, but the New Herald did.

I believe the it was in the Newspaper on June 4, 2004, and they took a photo and it was a big article about my books, and it was nice being in the newspaper, and then I was on Brian show cable TV, and I also had a interview, and at that time I had flyer and promote my books and I did some books signing event at Barnes and Noble and I did some good but not that great and then I did Books, bushes and boats, in New London, CT and I didn't sells any one book of mine and I was really upset, but I did build a website, and I did passed out my business card, and after my first book I published a lot of book afterward, and then sells them and I did accomplish my dreams about being a author, but I still had skeptic and make fun of me but I didn't care about them because alls my life, seems like someone was always making fun of me and they think I was not smart enough but I knew better that I was smart .

I join the group they are called Connecticut Authors and Publishers association and there meeting are held in Avon, Connecticut and I am a member, and they also did an article in there authority about me.

I think of myself has a under dog and so I think that I need to work extras hard to success, my goal, and then they had book event the Hartford library and I stuck out again because they place me in the wrong spot and no one didn't sees me.

Then I did a book event for the New Britain Youth, and I did sells some books and the title was A Polish Christmas story with the magical Christmas tree, and that was published in 2005 and much more book were published after that one, I was not finish writing I had more stories to tells.

Yes so let me go back when I was in the New Britain Herald and my sister mother in law and called up my sister and I she said your sister in the newspaper and then she said you must be proud of your sister and then my sister called and said, she was proud of me and then two day after I my sister took my book home and she asked who edited that Book, just a friend and they didn't do a good job for that book.

One day my mom and I when to Foxwoods and we when to played and then after dinner, we stop because the music was playing out of the buffet and that time I met Erik Narwhal and the Manatees, and I passed out my business card. Erik told the peoples about me and then my mom and I when to Ellis Con with Barbie and I sold a few copies of Father and Sons to Steve from the time machine and also No Ending Dreams to one person and that was a good day and then I did a another event in Plainville and it was for the gamer and I did the books signing event and I believe I sold two book at that event and then I join the march of the dimes and then I donate the book for the book fundraiser, and I also attended three time and one time I was a meet and greet person at the Connecticut convention in Hartford and one time I attended in Windsor, when I took a limo and my parents were worry about me and then Karen pick me up and took me home,. And then the other time I when with my friend, Rick. But before that time, I met Rick at my books signing event at Pepe Pizza on west middle turnpike, Karen and Ryan and then Ricky came and then we had pizza and I passed out my business card and I then Ricky and I spoke and I have seen him since 1991 and when he broke my heart and at that point I wanted to get even with him and he used me by taking money and I paying for the trip to Cape cod, and I was very angry at him and I did wanted to get even at that point and so Rick c did called and I couldn't make up my mind to called him back or not.

It took me about three days and then I called him and it was in Jan 2005, and he wanted to take me out and I told him that I was not ready.

But times when by and I did accept to sees him so we when decided to go to Applebec and so he somehow he lock his key in the car and we had to wait for triple a to come and unable the door for his car, then Rick C and got his keys and then we when inside the restaurant.

So at that time we got the table and we said separate check and then we waited for our foods to come and when I saw him that night he gave me a kissed on my lips and I gave a kissed too.

Then we when to the movie and we saw chain saw massacre and the beginning and it was some part, terrible and then after the movie,, Ricky ands I when to my house and he talked with my mom and dad and said he really didn't like that movie with bloods and bodies parts and then we sat in the kitchen and we talked and then he wanted to go upstairs to practice on the computer and at first we used the computer and then we had sex and then suddenly I got dizzy and Ricky had to hold me and I walk up the mirror and I notice the clock broke that moment and then I walks back to Ricky and he hold me and he told my mom and my mom when upstairs because I couldn't walks Ricky to the door and then he left and my mom stay with me for a while and then I fell asleep and I was fine, so

Sure I written songs and they got published and then I got my poetry published for a price and I do enjoy writing since junior high and there were moment that I just couldn't put into words and they were reverse and but I had friends that help me out and I did get a lot of books published, and everyone is proud of me, especially my mom and dad and the other in the family I don't think so, and it is a challenge for me to accomplished this dreams especially when peoples think that you are not normal.

I started to sees my ex boyfriend and we when to Ron and rolls for rolling skating and I tried it out and one day I fell and Karen helped me out and I just didn't do that again but I when to parties and it was nice to meet friends like Jenny and then Pam, and so I went with Ricky a lot and it was fun and a lot time that Ricky when to Rocky neck and first we stop at Subway and got a sub and then we headed there and then after the beach we make plan to sees a concert and the first one was Tom Jones and Ricky took me for my birthday and then after the concert we when to eat and then we gambling a little bit and then we when to Foxwoods and after Mohegan sun.

After the casino Ricky and I when to my house and we played cards and then we just talked about old times and then my dad was in bed and then my mom when to sleep and Ricky and I when upstairs and we had sex and he said " He loved it very much" and I said the same.

After that Ricky took a shower and so did I and then he when home.

When Ricky. got home and he gave me a called and said I am home and on my cell phone and then Ricky took to me to Chicopee for dancing on Friday night and it was good and Ricky bought me a beer and we dances all night long and then we did the electric slide and then Ricky dance with other persons and I just watched and then we when home and he left and there were many times that Dick took me to the single dance at the gallery and it was fun ands I met more persons and then that night Rick and I played more card games like 21 and rummy and then he said I am bored, and then left, and then he gave me a kissed and then said bye.

Went he got home and gave me called and then Ricky, and today was my birthday and Ricky called and sang Happy Birthday. Then Ricky asked if I wanted to go skating and I said not today, but at this time I was still angry at Ricky about hurting me in the past, and I wanted to get even in and I wrote letting and then I called Ricky not to opened it and then we were fine.

Ricky, and when to the Big E and we when after 5 pm and we when into the circus but it was late and we were not able to sees it and we kick out, and so we try to sneak in but we were unable too. Also I saw Donna Summer with Ricky and it was a lot fun and we also when to Foxwoods and stay out all night long and he like to be with me and I like being with Ricky too.

New Britain Museum of American arts 2005

Today I read the newspaper and I notice that Gene Wilder the actor and author will be showing his painting and also would have a book signing event at the museum and I told my brother to drive me to the museum that day on July 10, 2005 to Meet " Gene Wilder" and sees his painting and then I could be able to passed out my business cards to the peoples and too Gene Wilder, and the museum is in New Britain, Connecticut, and not too far from my home and they first had cocktail reception at the museum and I pays to get inside and then I stand with the crowds and waited for Mr. Gene Wilder to comes and he did and his wife Karen Wilder and she is very nice and friendly like Gene Wilder and after the cocktail reception, then it was the book signing event and so at first I thought maybe I will not buy the book and then Karen, Gene Wilder wife told me to come and meet her husband and I didn't wait in line and I shook his hand and I said nice too meet you and he said the same and then I decided to give him my business card and then, I thought it were be nice to have Gene Wilder, autograph so I purchase the book and Gene Wilder signed his signature and I was happy and then after the book event, Gene Wilder was showing his painting and then he was taking pictures with other peoples, so I ran into my neighbor and they took a picture of me and Gene Wilder that day and I was very happy that I when to his book event and he is very nice man and friendly and his wife too.

The event was about to finish and I had to called my brother but my neighbor said we will take you home and you don't need to called him so I got inside there car and we drove away from there and they got a few copies of Gene Wilder Books, and I thanks them for taking me home and they drop me off in my driveway and I when inside and I show my parents the book and the title of the book is called " Kiss me like a stranger my love and arts". Ands Gene Wilder, New/ Now Painting by Gene Wilder, it was nice meeting Gene Wilder and having a photo with him too.

That day I was really excited and happy that I when to sees Mr. Wilder and it was good to sees an actor that was in Silver streak and other movies.

Yes I shook his hand but I was not stalker and I know that he is an actor but I treated him has an ordinary man.

I will remember that day all my life that I met a famous person beside Betty Ford in 1989 at the Beverly center so I met two famous person so far in my life and got there book and I think that I became a writer because I got a signed book by "Betty Ford" and I do enjoy writing stories.

Since junior high and high school and I believe that I have a lot of stories to tell and I do enjoy writing and it was a good experience meeting a bestseller author and actor at the Beverly center and at the New Britain Museum, to inspire to become an author myself, and fulfilled my dreams. I couldn't believe that I met Betty Ford in 1989 and then Gene Wilder in 2005.

June 30, 2007

Today is June 30, I was not going to the firework this year to Manchester community college and so I am going with Karen and my mom and I are going to go too Foxwoods and so my mom was excited and we cannot wait to get there so, so we arrival and then Karen parked the car and then we walked to the lobby of the casino, and stop to get some foods and we when into the buffet and then we ate and then we started to walks and then played for a while and then we heard the music and it was "Erik Narwhal and the Manatees,, then we walks up the stair and then we sat down at the table and then about one minute later, Erik was looking for me to be there to thanks for putting him in the book, and I said I really like your music and I really enjoyed it and so put you in my book and so Erik is a very nice person and he has the talent and I just like when I sees him and so I do mention my friend Erik Narwhal and I told him that I was having a Fundraiser and he said he was coming and but I told him that I think that I couldn't afford to pays for everyone so, he didn't show up and I understood, and on that day, Erik came to the table and said I am glad to sees you and I said the same and then I said I really like your music and I asked if he had a CD and he said I will sees and few minutes later gave me two CD and also to my friend Karen.

After that Karen and I were dancing on the dance floor and it was fun but there was a different time that I felt that Erik was like avoid me, because he had a lot on his mind that day, and I do understand.

But on June 30, 2005 and he was not the same like the last time and he was very friendly to me. And then I told him more about my books and he said he was checking them out…. And I said that is great!

Also that night I was singing along with Erik and dancing and taking a drink of water and being hot after dancing…. And it was a great night and Erik said he were check out my new books and were asked a friend to help me with my website but I didn't contact Erik Narwhal, because he is too busy and working at clubs like main street café in London, CT and mostly in RI and so far I didn't have chance to go to sees him there, but maybe 1 one I will and so, then that evening I said bye to Erik we are leaving and going home and it was nice seeing you and hope too sees you again and we walk way and headed to the car and we when inside and we drove away from the Foxwoods and driving through the woods and I was showing Karen the ways out and then we got on 395 north and it seems it was taking that long to get home and we got home and I thanks Karen and also gave Karen for gas and it was nice time at Foxwoods and then Karen left and we told to her to called when she got home and my mom and I when inside and told my dad that we were lucky and we won some money and show my dad.

Also that year I attended a fundraiser at the Aqua turf to attend the special Olympic and I ran into Gary Craig and I also met Barbara Fowler that time and I asked the peoples that how can I donate my books and they explained and then I spoke a little to Gary Craig and then I ate the dinner and later that night my brother pick me up from the aqua turf and that night Gary Craig sang a song and then Barbara Fowler and got her CD and she signed and I was happy that I could help a cause for "Special Olympic" and met more peoples and gave them my business card and then I called and I when home and then I shown my mom and dad the CD and then I got change and when to sleep and I was happy I when to the fundraiser like to March of Dimes and then I attend one fundraiser I did a book event and one of my book were " A Polish Christmas Story with a magical Christmas tree" feature at the MIA old building for the New Britain Youth that at local on high street and Kensington Connecticut for wild life.

This benefit was on October 7, 2005, and I was the author of the night and they had a reception and then a silent auction and a grab bag and one of my book was include in the package, and after the fundraiser they gave me beautiful flowers and I think that I sold a few books that night and I receive cash, and then I waited for my brother to take me home and it was not too far from my house probably about five minute and I was home and I had to carry my books and my flowers in my hands and I met more peoples and more knew about my books and my website.

" This is my saying well one minute you are on stage and the next you are not… you need to believe in yourself and you need to be positive whatever you do in life and don't let someone to make you feel that you stupid of dumb and don't let them judge you,, and you don't even know you and in one case there was a time that I thought a muse of Connecticut were include me into her group but she denied me because she said I was not serious about my writing and how were she know, if I was serious about my writing she didn't even give me a chance but just blow me off and I don't forget that I was judge about not being prefect at that time but not giving a chance, that is not fair.

She refuse me has a member and said that I make a lot error in my work because at that time I had no one to help me so I had no choice but thing had change and I still I was treated unfair even from for trying to be on talked radio and she shot me down, and refuse me to be there and said I that I was a self publish author and they do not have that type of author on the show and I explained that I didn't print the book but author house and it is totally different and I thought that I was not good enough to be interview and once day I got discrimination from a person. Once again, unfair, but that is life and you have to deal with it.

In May 2007 I decided to go to Broadcasting school and I attend the open house about two weeks before classes began so I watched a video in the classroom and I answered the questions and then I filled out the forms and did a audition and then after my brother and my dad pick me up at the school and I think that I was accept, so I told my parent that I am going to broadcasting, but before I went to broadcasting school, I met Paul L with my friend on September 30, 2006 and Barbie pick me up from my house and then we when to get Peter and Ed and then we when to Hartford to the movie so Peter and Ed went to sees the movie the Johnny Depp movie and Barbie and I went to sees the 911 movie, and after we saw our movie and it was finished early so we snuck in and saw the other movie and after that Peter asked me if I wanted to go out with Him and I said yes.

After the movie finished we headed to the car and Peter said why you don't take us to dinner Barbie, but Barbie said well we will stop for ice cream in West Hartford and is that ok and Peter said fine.

Later when we arrival to my house, Peter said I will give you a called at that time Peter had my cell number and not my house number and then, I started to sees Peter and Ed took me to Milford and we had a early Happy new year. So let go back, yes I got accept to broadcasting school and I was very happy about that, and before that I was at the Big E on September 2006 and it was good and also I met Delores and Mark and so let me tell you my new friend, she is a friendly and she has dark hair and she is tall and medium build and her husband is slim and tall and about 5 8 tall and very nice and friendly too.

The first year of the Big E Delores and Mark came over to gets more of my Christmas story books, and they sat and waited me to bring the books down and they spoke to my parents and then I gave them the books and they left.

On my day of the big e my friend Barbie bought there and then, I think that we saw Taylor Hicks for a concert, but I am sure of the date and year.

Delores and I became good friends and we go out for lunch and sometime.

Every day I drove to bird eyes to the broadcasting school and I when there four times a weeks, and teacher like John and Neal and other teacher and we did alls different project and then we had a final exam that we had to do news and reported so that time I was a an association producer and that day was graduation on September 7, 2007 and it was a Friday and my parents didn't go and I was alone and I had no one really talking to me, and that day we receive our broadcasting certificate and it was great and we had pizza and it really when fast and I met a lot new friend like Marty and Barbara and I was happy and then after that I went to studio time and but I never learned how to cut a CD and make an audition tape to get a job and so I when to Keith and he said it is really difficult if you don't drive on highway.

On July 11 2007 we when to New York City to sees a taping of Monte William show and I was really excited about that time and I met our students that graduate sooner and later than I and it was very interest that day I drove in the morning and park the car in the parking lot and everyone was waiting for the bus to comes and than I check the car if it was lock and then I sat on the bus and everyone got on and then we were headed to New York city and I was happy and then they put on a movie and alls the ways there, and when we got there, they parked the bus and then we got out and we had to stay in the line and then they open the door and passed out the tickets to us and we enter into the building and stay for awhile in the waiting room.

About half hour later, and then we enter the studio and then got our seat and the they had some fun games before, and the show started, and we saw the two show taping and then we got a signed picture of Monte William and when on the bus and they gave us more pizza for the road and I just had two piece of the pizza and that day I was hungry, and we were getting near to the parking lot of the school and when we arrival into Connecticut it was rainy and I was a bit worry and so it was a little dark and then I waited for everyone to leave and then I backed up after the bus left and then I left the school parking lot and headed home, and I put on the light and I got to five corner and then I the light turn green and I was on ways home and then more lights and then on one dark road, somehow I hit the tree and but I was fine and then I turn on a Slater road and soon turning on Scarlett and I was home and turn into the driveway and I was home and I was relief and safe and I told my mom and dad and but before I when inside I check the car and it was ok.

About one week later I when for studio time and I visit my friend Barbara and said hello and then I stay for awhile.

Also I told my friend Ricky that I was doing studio time and I probably will intern for 96.5 and he was happy for me.

So that time I drove back and forward and then I just stop and the weather was not that good and I didn't know how to drive in snow or sleet.

So time when by and I when to the dentist in October 2007 to get my filing and he put the filing and then it was ok when I got home and it was fine, and then later it started to give me pain and so more pains, and I was really painful and I couldn't reach my dentist, but I did leave the message and the dentist got back to me and also I pays over a hundred dollar for the first dentist, and then I make the appointment on Thursday and then that day I when to get that tooth pull out and the dentist wanted to know that how will I pays for it and then there was on the form that it was a risk, and then I signed and then I had to give them the check and then they took me into the room and then, he gave me a needle into my tooth and they hold me back and then my tooth was pull out and then I when to my dad and then we went to the car and then on the ways home I felt hot and then I thought I was going to passed out so my dad put on the air condition and they also gave me a prescription for my pain and I was not able to go because I felt so hot after getting that tooth pull out and on the ways home I saw white lights alls the ways home and I was really at that moment I thought I would passed out, and I was really scare that day, and that day I stay in bed and I didn't eat neither. That was the worst experience that I had from the dentist at that point I thought I was going to end up in the hospital and but I didn't but few days I couldn't eat and I was having a lot problem and think that the dentist should asked you if your filing didn't hurt and then fix it but he didn't and that why I had the problem and it was unfair that I paid twice for the hurt and pain and being very sick, and make sure that you asked your dentist what he is doing before he starts the job on you, in case you might end up in the emergency room.

When I got out of the car, my dad hold me and walks me into my parents room and put on the air condition and then my boyfriend Peter called and asked how I was doing and he said that he was worry about me.

At that time I need to eat foods like pudding and Jell-O, that kind of food.

There was a time that I told Ricky that I been kidnap by Peter and it was not true and I somehow he was worry about me,

So I send Ricky a card and said I was held hostage by Peter and Ricky thought I was in danger, so Ricky called the orange police about me being danger. So I answered the phone and I told the police officer I was fine, and about half hour the New Britain, CT. about ten minutes later the two police cars, and I went outside to my mom, and I spoke to the police officer and told him that day I went Grove hill clinic, so that morning I felt fine and when we arrive to the clinic, then I felt a little sick, I started to have a backache and fainted feeling that I would passed out. About twenty minutes my parents had there blood test, and then we left but my mom and dad hold me until that day, I was not hungry and I did not calls Ricky and I was not in danger and I am fine. Then the officer written what I was saying and my mom and I went inside and they left. About one hour later I called Ricky and tell him that I was ok! But Ricky was not home, he was headed to the Halloween party, so I called that person that had the party and tell Ricky that I am fine. Since that day Ricky he was angry at me and didn't speak to me since that incident.

That night I was worry if I would be able to go to Peter, because I was feeling that well that night. But the next morning I felt fine and so Karen show up and I went into her car and we headed to West Haven, to his apartment and I bought the potatoes salad and at I was afraid to eat but I did and I was fine and than we went Denny, about two hours later we left and Peter gave me a kissed and we drove off and headed home.

There was a time that I took the train from Berlin to New haven and to see my boyfriend Peter, and Peter didn't pick me up from the station so I had to take the taxi cab and pays about $10.00 dollars, and I crossed the street, then I opened the door and I went inside and buzzed him but he didn't let me in and someone let in and took the elevator to the second floor and knock at the door, said hello Jean Marie, and I went inside.

Then there was a time that I was in Peter class and I and I had to speak in front of class at Southern college and I believe I did well and they like me.

Later that night Peter drove me home but I went to his class that day got bitten by my dog Susie and Peter was in my room and using my computer and using my printer and I believe that somehow Peter broke my computer and it would not work right, ever since.

The whole incident started went Peter that morning, Peter sat down at the kitchen table and read the newspaper and my feeding the dog, and Susie was finished and dad tried to take the bowl.

Then Susie bite my dad and my dad went to the doctor and it was not bad.

About five hours later my brother came from work and I told him what happened and then I left and we would on our way to southern and I was doing sign language to my brother, and said bye and went into the car and we drove off in the black Cadillac. Peter and I went to the movie that night.

I remember the time that Karen and I and Liz and we headed to Rocky neck and we stop at the pizza place and had a slice pizza and soda and after that we would headed to the beach, and we got to the beach and Karen parked the car and got our stuff, and walk under the bridge and into the beach and we lay the blanket and sat down and looking at the ocean.

We stay for awhile and then bug started to bite us so we decided to leave and we decided to go to diary queen for ice cream that night Karen stay overnight at my house and Susie was watching us and stay all night and the next morning I notice that papers would on the floor.

Then my mom gave Karen some breakfast and coffee and the next day we met up with Liz and that day we went to the movie.

To sees momma MIA. After the movie we when to Wendy for lunch.

Later that day Karen took me home and Liz went home and left she left and I went inside and I said bye.

There was a time that Karen and I went to the gallery and Karen met a man and they started to John and that night she danced and talked with him.

But I sat alone and I didn't dance with anyone just watched and there was a time that Timmy was there and we danced Karen and I and

Timmy, and it was fun that night and there was a time that Peter went with me and he asked if Karen could borrow money for the dance, and I had to pays her back and Peter didn't pays me back, ever since. Also Peter danced with me and Karen that night and it was fun then Peter said he didn't have money for gas, that night that I felt that Peter was using me and then he drop me home and then he left and I didn't know where he went to unknown location.

Also there was a time that I went to the gallery with Karen and other friends and ran into Ricky, said I would take her home, but I would like have about $20.00 to take her home and at time we all said no ways!

So that we agree and I said no I am going home with Karen and about two hours later we left the gallery and then Karen took me home and I got into the car and when inside the car and drove way into the road and then into the highway, and then I got home and I got out of car and when inside and I said bye to Karen and she drove away and headed up the hill and when home.

Then there was an other incident that Karen and I had to move Peter stuff to his mom to Orange from Milford and at that time Peter moved to Maine and so he wanted me to help him out and so that time Karen had a truck and Peter said that he were pays Karen, but he never did but I pays her, and there would times that we missed the road to his mom house.

So that night Karen and I went about three times and then we stop for coffee at the Mc Donald and we met Peter mom and Susan that time and Peter mom was very nice and said did I meet you before I said you, this is the first time tonight, and then we said we got to go and then we left and that night I gave Karen a check for the move and I felt it was unfair because I was not the one that was moving but I still paid her.

One day I invited Karen and Ryan and Timmy to comes over swimming and then Barbie and Ed too, and that time that Karen was looking for a boyfriend and he his name was Nick, and he lived in Pennsylvania, and it was near Lancaster, PA, and Timmy told her to go and meet him and Karen said agree with him so she booked a motel near intercourse and then she said I am going and when I get close I will called Nick, so Karen decided to meet that guy Nick, I remember that day when I check up Karen and Nick were at the restaurant for dinner and I spoke to him, and he seems nice.

I also remember the time that Timmy came over because he needed to used my computer and so I let him and then he thought he broke my computer because I didn't have flopping disk on my system and he was looking for work at that time and after that we when for dinner at "Town and Country" and he said wow this place is expensive. But I said it is good.

I remember the time that I met Karen parents around her brother birthday and his uncle, and we when to a buffet and they treated me and it was very nice of them and I did thanks them and then later that night Karen took me home and Karen called me and then I spoke with her again, and about the time that we had to go to West Haven to pick up Peter and take him to the casino and he spoke more to Karen than me. And then Peter gave my mom some carnations in the car and mom and Peter sat together in back of Karen car and it seems long before Peter came to car but we didn't says anything at times.

Before we left West Haven we stop at Burger king for soda, that what Peter wanted and but that days was extremely long and it was going to the casino and going back to Peter place that was a long drive, and Karen did a big favor for me to sees my boyfriend, after that Peter got a car and then he travel to me and I was saw him or I took the train to sees him.

But a lot times I had take the taxi cab because he was like taking nap or just wanted me to pays more money that I didn't have.

Also I time I had to buy him lunch and I thought it was not right and also pays for gas I felt used that day.

Now Peter started that he needed to move away from West Haven and need to move elsewhere and he cannot stay her and I don't have enough money to live in Connecticut and so Peter decided to move to Fitchburg Mass.

So he asked Barbie and Ed to move him from West haven to Fitchburg and so Barbie and Ed came to pick me up and we headed to West Haven for his move and so that day I had packed his clothes and then we had to pack the car, so that day I ended up to be with Peter headed to Fitchburg.

When we arrival there Barbie and Ed were there and they were ready to unpack the van and bring the stuff into Peter apartment and so I kind of help but I was not that strong like Barbie and Ed and Peter, so I climb a few times but then I stand at the van and took stuff out and then I when upstairs and took stuff out of his suitcase and put inside the closet.

After that I took a walks around the side of the house and I told Peter that is very slippery and be careful and about ten minutes, Barbie and I and Ed looked and Peter said I have fell there and I think that I broke my elbow and that night, I called 911 and then my cell when out and I called again and then we told them to pick up Peter at friendly and then we waited until the ambulance came and then we left Peter alone but Ed wanted to follow the ambulance and Barbie refuse and said I have to gets up early for work and I don't want to spend all night in the hospital and so left Peter in the parking and he was enter the ambulance and we headed to Connecticut.

Then Barbie said maybe you should have stay with your boyfriend and I said how were I gets home and plus I need to take care of my mom and dad with there medicines.

Later that night we arrival to my house and Barbie drop me off and I when inside and then they left and then I called Peter on his cell phone I couldn't reach him but I tried a few times, I believe that Peter thought it was my fault but I didn't tell him to there at night but at a different time.

But Peter just got hurt the first night that he moves to Fitchburg.

Then about two days later Peter called and said to my mom, would I be able to stay at your house for two weeks and my mom said where were you sleep? And Peter said at Jean Marie room and where would she sleep on the couch and but my mom said sorry we don't have the room and one night he stay at Linda house but she didn't want him there neither.

After that incident, Karen and I went to visit Peter and we when to WALMART to buy shades and to cover up the windows and Karen put them up and then we when to eat at a place like friendly and it was extremely expensive and I had to paid for the meal for Peter, and then we took him home and we left Fitchburg and then we headed to Connecticut, and then we plan to go to the gallery to dance. At that time, Peter had two surgeries for his elbow, and he wanted attended Fitchburg University and he was passing his grades, and soon he was going to graduation, but something bad happened and they said that he was a stalker at the school and they had a hearing.

Also Peter had to leave Fitchburg because a bad snow storm came and he had to leave and he when to Maine to see Clark.

One time that Karen and I when to visit Peter one more time and this time we when to buys shower curtain, then Karen put up the curtain and about two hour later, and we went home.

Now Peter was worry that he were not get his diploma, but he did receive and now it was time for Peter to move from Fitchburg and move to Worcester, Mass, and at that time his friend Clark came and move him to that place on near Pelham and on the third floor and then there was an incident that sounded that Peter was suicide about his face and it was in the email, so I asked my friend Barbie and told me to called the police and that was a big mistake of my part.

So it was lucky that Peter was not home because about twenty police arrival and storm into his Place and broke his door and scare the landlord, and at that time, Peter was very rude and means and said maybe I should have never talked too you, so I still remember how means he was too me and I do care for him and he was really abusing and mean, and that day I really cried and apology trying to help him out and now I know better.

Then there was an other incident his friend Donna, when she had a argument with her mom and Peter at that point thought that she were killed herself so he called the special line to and that night Donna was very angry what Peter did, and she started to called him names and didn't want to talked with him, and then Peter thought it that he had to send her card, but he never send me a card or not even flowers.

Now I need to tell you about the times that I when to the big e and I met famous peoples like Taylor Hicks and Mickey Dolenez and it was a great experience and also I was doing a books event and sold a lot of books, and met a lot of fan. So now I need to tell you about the time that I went to Pennsylvania, with Karen and I met her new friend Cookie and I hope that I didn't repeating myself but she enjoy watching the hallmark movies and then after watching the movie and then we when back to the conform inn and then the next day, we took a long ride through the "Amish county" and saw the horse buggy and then we when to into the store, and pick up the jelly and then we had lunch. We also went to the " Green Dragon" and pick up whoopee pie and headed back to cookie place and then we said bye and we when to back to the motel, because tomorrow we will be going home and then Peter gave me a called and then I talked with him a while and then I when to sleep.

Beside hang out with Karen, I when places with Delores and Mark and we when to Mohegan sun and we played a little and then we when home and then, Mark and Delores, said Peter said nice too meet you, Mark and Mark and Peter talked for awhile and then we when to our room on the 21 floor and then I put on the TV and Peter said turn that off and I did.

When I was changing, right in front of the mirror and he said I see everything and tried too but he still sees it.

At that time we slept together but nothing did happened, so it was good.

We also went to the concert to sees the moody blues, and Peter was dancing in the aisle.

The next foods when for lunch and I had a foods coupon for seventy five dollars and I order three pizzas and one we ate at restaurant and then we were headed home, and then he asked about my vision and I told him but I don't predict the future and he wanted to know about Sam, and told him and then, Sam said don't listen to Jean, and so Peter didn't know what to says or believe at that point so I kept quiet and I don't I want that Peter were have a panic attack at that moment.

But back to Donna, it was month and month before she spoke to Peter.

Events

In 2008 once again I had book event and when on short trip with Karen to Pennsylvania, and so we decide to go during the fourth of July and it was fun and we went to burger king and then we when to the green dragon, and we had a good time and Karen got whoopee pies and we when to the store for water and sodas and when back to the hotel and took walks that day. Also we when on the same road and asked Amish farmer to get on the right road and but we got on the same road for few times and I was really scared that day, but we got safe back to the hotel and I was very happy about being safe and not lost but I tried not too show it but I was really scare that day .Time for the anniversary party at my Connecticut authors and publishers party in Avon and I did asked Peter and he refuse so I asked my old friend,. Ricky to comes with me and the party was on March 21, 20008 and my friend Ricky came and pick me up and we had a six pack and then we when inside and said hi to one of the member and then we at the table and then Ricky put the beer to keep it cold and then we sat on the other side of Delores and Mark and then there a guy name Dale, and he was with his family and I introduce to my friend Ricky and we sat and listen to the speaker and then we were serve foods and then it was night of dancing.

The party ended at 9 pm and I said hello to Delores and Mark and I told Ricky, that is the author of Truth never changes and he shook his hands and then we left and Ricky decided to take me to Chicopee and we when to place to dance, and there were times that I thought, Delores was mad at me and I was wrong, and I also remember when I bought my new book Lust, love and sex and pleasure and I show it to Delores and Kathy and then she said how can you write this time of book, but I guess of my experience.

But in my mind I thought they were making fun of me but I was wrong.

But Kathy couldn't believe what I written in the book, and then by soon that Spooky was going to get published by Publish America, and my edited was Karen, and she did my other book and I knew she was a professional editor for my books. Karen also edited my other book A Drama queen collides with Prince charming and her son help out and I was happy about the book.

Yes I did a lot self published book because I wanted my reader to read my stories and I did also accomplish my dreams.

So I started to hang out with Delores from CAPA and then we when to Olive garden for lunch and we sat there for hours and hours at that time I was thinking about rewrite the Christmas story with the magical Christmas tree but we didn't come up with new material and title so, we just didn't do that project. But Delores also helped me out for CAPA U and with my query letter to the agent and I once again strike out.

I told Delores that I am not going to spend that money and I didn't learned anything from that university and I was very disappoint about that.

But Delores, help me out with my poster that I used for the big E and that year was a good year and I sold about 30 books that year and I make good money, so talking about that why don't I tell you before I met Peter and I went with Ricky to the Christmas party, at the free spirit.

Then I went a lot to Ron and Roll and then I when to there Halloween party and I had a lot time but one time I started to choke and Ricky help me out and I was all right! After the party I when home and then Ricky stay for awhile and we talked about things and he I know him over thirty years.

Ands doing the Big E the second year was really exciting and I met a lot of peoples and I sold a lot of books and that day we left early because Ed came along before that we when to Sam club because he thought he lost his wallet but he didn't and then when he found it and we were on our ways.

Then we stop at friendly for breakfast and then we headed, to the big e.

And after the big e, left and headed home and my mom and dad were surprise that we came about 6pm that night and one time I did the big e on a Sunday and it was good and I knew that I were not be afraid of the mails that I was receiving and it was good., and we got home and Barbie and Ed drop off and I went inside and I said bye and I talk with Barbie later and then I got change and watched some TV, yes in the past I did have a little episode of vertigo but not that bad. But it didn't last long disappear.

One time that I was invite to Timmy Birthday party and it was really bad outside and I Karen and her boyfriend were running late, and I believe it were been better if Karen left me home instead of taking me to the party, because that Timmy had to take me home and it was slippery and he had to take me home and I felt bad and angry at the same time and I cannot explained it at this moment, I would not like to be in that situation again.

About the time that we when to the casino that Karen and her boyfriend didn't even looked back if we were all right and my mom she couldn't walks that fast neither and I was worry that they could have left us at the casino and the restaurant that we ate I didn't like the foods, and it was expensive.

I will never forget that night and I didn't win and I we just when home broke and just wants to forget about that night and then we got home and they drop off and we when inside the house and so I talked with Karen the next day.

So there were other incident that Peter make me cried and said you don't know how to put air for a tire and I said no and he was rude and means toward and called me a idiot and I started more and he was really abuse and I didn't want to be near him and then there was a incident when Barbie and Ed and I and Peter when to the New Britain Diner and he got called on his birthday March 15 and he got one called from his cousin from Florida and he didn't mention his girlfriend " Jean Marie" and when he got off the phone Barbie really started to says things that went out of control and Peter also said that he didn't want to get marry and Barbie said to Me and said you should find someone that wants to get marry and treat you well, and before that I started to choke on water and really panic and Barbie and Ed and Peter didn't notice about few minute later and then Barbie told me to relax and I did and I got better and then we had our food and Ed had a polish dish and after dinner we left the restaurant and I still was crying and Peter said stop behaving like a child and then said Peter said I don't want to be in the same room with Barbie because we don't get along and I said fine.

That night Peter drove me home and then he took off to unknown location and then there was a time that Peter suppose to comes over and he stood me up and said I am not cheating on you and he apology to me so many times.

Then there are holiday like Easter said I will be coming over but first I need to take a nap, and at the point I thought he were comes, about two hours later he change his mind and he said that he ended up at the hospital. So I felt hurt one more times about Peter.

You must be thinking I do have a complication relationship with Peter and it will be four year this September 30, and I think that he forgot and about it , but I will not tells him but I met be a little furious about his personality is not that great social with Peoples, but it did approve a bit.

So when I don't see my boyfriend Peter, I see my friends like Delores and Mark and Ed and Barbie and Billy, and we go out for dinner, and it was good to be out with them.

Once in awhile visit my sister and I also work for my sister to take care of the aunt and I drove when they were doing the pavement on the road and it was not easy especially on Corbin and West Main Street in the afternoon and the school buses and then the light and the bump. When I did the babysitter job I sat over my sister house and my sister bought me Pizza and once my nephew the same and aunt did not like that foods and said I want Chinese foods so my nephew order pizza and then Chinese foods and when to get it.

After dinner about two hour later I put her to bed and I when into my sister bedroom and I when to watched TV and called my mom and said everything is under control.

The next morning I woke up and then got dress and gave the aunt her breakfast and then I waited for my sister and my brother in law to get home from the casino.

There was a time that Karen and I when to Lancaster Pennsylvania and we got lost and I was really scared and we ended up on the same road and then we when to the farm and asked the nice Amish farmer and told us how to get out of the area and at one point I didn't want to tells Karen that I was about to panic and didn't want her to do the same, and then we when to the hotel and the next day I bought strawberry and then we bought candies on the ways home and I believe on this trip we took our own sandwiches and drinks to save, and that was a good ideas.

But most of the trip I don't eat much and that day we called Peter and my cell were going down and then when I got home and then we found out that one of Karen friend was in the Hartford hospital, and we went to sees him.

One of the person said are you his mother and I felt that was an insult and I am not an old lady, and I was probably younger than that person that was in the hospital, and then Karen took me home and Karen left and when home to Ryan, and at that times Karen and I hung out a lot and we when to the gallery and we when to the casino and then we when to the beach with our friend Timmy and sometime with Lucy and also we when to sees hairspray with Karen and Liz and Karen slept twice at my house and it was good.

I also went to birthdays and other occasion of Karen family things.

Now I was hanging with Delores and Mark and I stay out late and I when to there home and I had dinner and I when places like to New Hampshire, to pick up his books and I also receives boxes from that place and now I am using those boxes every time I am at the Big E, and Delores and Mark are the one that runs that fair, ok so let me talked about my books, well I have mystery man and then thin ice zombies in LA, and then I have Ricky Black and Jeanne Silk, and then I have willow lakes haunting, and mysterious nights and I hope that I am not repeating myself, and then Spooky, and it was publish by Publish America and that is my later book and I do enjoy write, I have my website and I met a lot famous peoples and I donate my books for March of Dimes and I MS.

In July 15, 2007 my book title DETOUR was on the bestseller list on Barnes & Noble and I was surprise and I didn't know that book was going to be a popular lists, and I told my friends about that and my other like Polish Christmas Story and thin ice was on the list and at that time I got more excited, and telling a story about my family and it is a story about my mom when she was growing up and how they had there Christmas tradition, and I just thought that were been a good book to write, and Germany invaded Poland about my dad and I thought Peoples were like to know about my dad that was born inn Radom Poland and how the German took him away from his family to work for the German during world war 2.

I feel right now I passed the seventeen book and I was not finished writing my book and I continue to published more books.

Also I tried to promote my books everywhere I could think of and even when I went to restaurant and even to the movie, and casino and on my website and my BLOG, and now on Face book.

I also have a series, and it is called No Ending Dreams.

So back to real world, went my mom when to the hospital and her legs were hurting and I was really worried and the doctor didn't help much and so but my mom visit a few times and then she saw a doctor at the clinic and said that was Arthritis and they gave her medicine and they harm her heart and that cause heart trouble but did help her with the legs problem but cause a different problem and it is not worth it.

One time my mom went to the hospital, and the doctor and said what are you doing here again and she was very fresh doctor and the nurse try to be nice and then told her to go else and then my mom got release and my brother pick us up and we went home and my mom was waiting for us and my dad open the door and said what did the doctor said, and we told my dad said what did the doctor said and we told my dad and then my mother change.

Then there was a time that my dad hurt his rib and they did XRAY and a lot morphine and stay for awhile and then got release, and we headed home and so far we had a doctor name Catherine, and she take care of my dad and she was a good doctor and she move further and my dad refuse to go there and so we change doctor and that was wrong, I mean it was a big mistake.

About me I so I hang out with Delores and Mark and so we spend a lot time and going places and I do have a lot fun with my friend and once again, it was the big E and I was happy about it but that day it was rainy and it was really mudding and then there was time that I when with Delores to help out with the books and I told my mom to make sure that she take the mail, boys! That days was the rude in my life but I don't want to really explains, I knew that secrets were come out but I thought they were not, but I thought I would be safe but when my brother got the mail and he was shock and he was angry and furious and almost crying and then I text him and explains that was dad, so then he cool off and my parents thought that maybe one of friends stole his identify, and I said no ways, and make this story short, I just messes up and I didn't want to hurt anyone and I do hate about lying too.

So I promise that I will not do that never again.

So on the ways home we stop at a pizza place and we wanted to eat and we decided on Pizza, boys! It was a surprise because it was the worst pizza that we ever had and so we ate some and then on the ways home, Delores stop near the woods and some wild animal ate our worst pizza and then Delores drove me home and I explained to my brother it was not his and everything is fine and my mom question who have did that too your brother and I said I don't know and my dad looked at me like I was the one and the next day was much better and in few day it will be the Big E and it was Barbie and I and Barbie, had her cell phone and when I was finish with book signing, and we walks around and watched the parade and then when for foods and then we when back to the Connecticut building pick up my poster and then we headed home around 6pm that day and I told my mom and dad I sold a lot of polish Christmas story and the other books.

On Halloween we purchase a lot candies but a lot children didn't comes to our home and then about 9 pm the light when off and then Halloween was over and we continue to watched the movie and then there is another holiday coming and it is thanksgiving and Peter is coming for thanksgiving and we are going my sister house and we are going to have thanksgiving at her house, so Peter will comes over and I will go with Peter and my parents will go with my brother and we will meet up there.

Meanwhile Susie will be home alone and my mom is worry how Susie will behave because she is not use too it, so my mom is a little worry about that.

It is about noon and Peter arrival and we were ready to leave but Peter and I left and Peter and I were on the road to my sister and we got there about that same time, so we got inside and my brother in law said nice too sees you again and Peter and sat together and then my parents came and then we eat the turkey and then my mom said to my dad and brother that we should go and they got up and they didn't even have the pumpkin pie or cheese cake so they left and Peter and I stay and then Peter when into the piano and played it and we stay for awhile and then we had some pie and then we left and Peter took me home and then he left to unknown. But he never tells me, and I don't ask, because he was not telling me.

On November 29, my mom started to have chest pain and we had to take her to emergency room and so I stay with my mom all night and morning and then on Sunday November 30, my mom didn't want to stay in the hospital because they were not doing anything at that point but they said she were not be able to leave but my mom signed a release and left and before that the doctor describe a prescription and my mom left and then that day I when to Mohegan Sun with Peter to sees the beach boys, but I was stupid that I didn't get the medicine before I left to the casino, that night, she was started to have chest pain but no medicine and I text my brother and asked how is mom and he told me that mom was having chest pain and the concert was not over and then it was and I told Peter and he contact the doctor and he spoke to him and so did I and we headed home has fast has we can, and we got home and Peter left and my brother and I when to CVS and we got the medicine and then my mom felt better and then the next day I suppose to called the doctor but the doctor called us and my mom went to sees him and the other doctor and then they remit her into Dempsey hospital for the surgery and at that point I was very worry and then about two hours later my mom was out of surgery and I called my dad and then my brother came and saw my mom but my dad stay home with my dog Susie.

Ands the next day my mom got release from the hospital and they gave my mom what to eat and what not to do, and we follow to the letter.

But soon it was going to be Christmas Eve but my brother took care of it but my mom still cooks the mushroom and cabbage soup and we had pickle herring and rye bread and the wafer, and Peter came late, and ate less.

Later that night Peter left and then we open up our gifts and then we kept it under the tree and then the next day we were going to my sister house for Christmas there. Well Peter came early to my house and took a short nap and later Peter and I when to CVS and he purchase chocolate for my sister and brother in law and we were on our ways there, and I saw my parents on Corbin Ave but Peter and I were just getting into the car so now Peter started up the car and now we headed to my sister house and my parents were inside and they are eating shrimp, so first sat down and then I got up and had some shrimp and sat on the chair and meanwhile Peter was eating near the counter and bugging my sister and brother in law and they are getting furious with him but not showing it too him and later that day my sister took me on the side and told me not too stay too long because of Peter and I said ok.

About half hour later my mom and dad and brother left because of the dog and then Peter and I left and Peter drop me off and then he headed to home to Fitchburg, and I when inside and change and then talked with my parents about Peter and how he behave this time and it was not good.

Time when by and it was going to be Happy New Year, so our family was together and Peter did called and I thought he were be with me because he is my boyfriend, but he didn't even shown up, and we watched Dick Clark and with Ryan Seacrest, and then the ball drop and it was 2010 and my dad gave my mom a kissed and then my mom gave my dad a kissed and said hope that you lives 100 year and then my dad gave my brother a handshake and then we had some soda and then my dad when to sleep and then I when upstairs and when to sleep.

The new year we had lamb and mash potatoes and vegetable and my boyfriend didn't even gave me a called, so it is a new year and what will it be a new year, but time will tells and in couples day my brother when to work and then so we did the normal stuff like going to the store and buys foods and then on Feb 3, 2010, and my mom said why don't you cancel your appointment with the dentist and I said no I am going and I didn't know what was going to happened to me at the dentist office, and I was waiting and then I when into the examine room and sat on the chair and then he put the switch so far I was ok and then something happened, I started to feel dizzy and now I was having vertigo and I didn't stops and then the dentist called my family doctor and they make the appointment for that day of the dentist but my dad suppose to sees the skin doctor but I had to cancel the appointment, and I saw my family doctor and then they make the appointment with the nose and ear doctor and I hardly could walks that day and I called Delores and told her what happened and she couldn't believe it and then I had a appointment on Feb 18, and I when into the office and they said sorry we make the appointment with the wrong doctor so you have to comes back another time, that day my brother took me but we when home and I have to wait for the other time, and then on Super bowl, I went to visit Peter and Karen took me and she really took care of me, went we when for pizza, she hold me from car too the restaurant and then I was waiting for my order my and again it occur and I told Karen what happened and then we got there and I realize that I had to climb a lot stairs to reach his third floor with climbing upstairs and then we reach his floor and we knock at the door and then Peter answered and then I took the seat and near the table and I had my own ice tea but Peter gave Karen lemonade and she had some and we stay for a while and then Peter mention that he wanted to go for the walks and I said not today maybe a other time and then we walks down and then Peter came down with us and then we left and we when home and I did text my brother and I asked him did he want pizza for super bowl and what size and went we were near I order the pizza and the eggplant grinder for Karen and then we when to pick it up and then we were on the ways to my house and so far I was ok but when I got out of the car I barely could walks once again Karen came to the rescue.

I when inside and Karen follow and I took a seat and my mom asked how I was doing at that time that great, and Karen stay for while and we share some pizza with Karen and about one hour later, Karen left and I went to change into my night clothes and then watched some TV but I felt not right yet. About one week later I saw the nose and ear doctor and he told me that I have partial vertigo with crystal in my ear and I need to sees the physical therapy and I need to cure my vertigo and I were be able to drive the car and on Feb 26, 2010 I saw the physical therapy and Delores took me and she asked if my mom or dad wanted to comes and they said no.

So that day, I had to tilt my head and gave me alls different kinds of tests and then she told me to lay down on the floor and I refuse and then I said I agree, to go on the chair and so she tilt me on the right and it was ok and then on the left and suddenly I got dizzy and I close my eyes at that point and I didn't know that you suppose to keep your eyes open.

But for few second I was so dizzy and I got scared so then the therapy, and I relax and I was fine and she make the appointment too see her and then I didn't go back again, because I got better after that therapy and I started to go places but their were moment it happened a little and then I got better and then at some point I couldn't wash my hair and that got better too.

Soon Feb was going be gone and I was going to do the books signing at the Millrace book in Farmington, CT and Mark was worry that I were be canceling out but I didn't, and I did shown up but I was still not prefect and the date was March 7, 2010 and I was going to talked about Poison pen so I ended up telling the story how I became a author and I started to cried, and I told them about Gary how he died and how I written the book about him and the memories.

Then I told then that sometime I write in reserve and then I had a disability, and they listened to me and then the other speaker and then one of the person when out to his car and asked if I could signed the book to Jessica and Ron and I said yes of course and it make me very happy and that day was good and later Delores and I went to Mohegan Sun because we had free plays.

After the casino Delores took me home and I said I will talked with you later and we both played games on Face book and I really like playing mafia and café and but I use too play more games, and so I also enjoy watching movies and most of alls horror flick, and comedy, that I really like.

About two weeks later will be Easter, on good Friday the priest will comes and bless the foods and we don't eat meat on good Friday, so far I think that Peter will be coming for Easter, and on Easter day Peter called that he will take a nap and he will comes over, but then he said that he didn't feel good and my sister didn't come neither because she just came back from work and my brother in law and nephew came and it was nice and later that day I called my friend Ricky and he came over and had some ham and kielbasa and then a little later we when to the " Free spirit" and I met a DJ Rick and he was very nice and he talked with me and dance with me too and I passed out my business card, and later that day, after the dance we when to Chicopee and dance more and I called my mom not to worry and then after that I came home so did Ricky, and he stay a while. On my dad birthday we got a cake at big y and my dad like it very much and we sang happy birthday and he just turned 89 year old.

My dad like working in the garden and helping my brother with pool but it was not time to open the pool, yet. But my dad like to rake the leaves and sit at the picnic table and talked with my brother who is deaf and my dad did understand my brother sometime and sometime I had to explain.

One day before mother day and I when to CAPA U with Mark and Delores and this year once again I met a agent and I did get a little luckier and still working on that book, and I met Jake and he came up to the table and asked if he can sit next too me and I said yes. We talked for a while and we exchange phone number and then I said bye and I walks to Mark and Delores and Delores and said we are going to Border book after this event and I said ok and we were going to sees some guy name foxy.

Foxy is a musician that play keyboard and sing John Lennon songs and at first we when there and the manger didn't know what we were talking about and then we said that we would come back after dinner and we when to friendly and then we when back to border and at that time foxy was singing a crowds.

We walks in and sat down and listening to Foxy and he was great and we also purchase his CD and also mark and I gave our book and signed too him.

Also he came up to us and sang a song to us and it was really a lot of fun and later that night we said bye and we drove ways and we didn't sees him and we will wait until comes back to the east coast again.

In June 4, 2010, we were invited to graduation to Peter massage in Mass, and at first I didn't know if I was going because I still had vertigo and I was really worry but my boyfriend convince me to go and he asked his good friend Eddie to take me and so I said yes and on June 4, 2010, and Eddie pick me up and noon and we were headed to the graduation and I had map quest and he said he wanted to comes much earlier in case that we got lost but we didn't and we got there about three hours earlier and then we when inside the restaurant and we sat down and we order the ice cream and watch the river with the boats and I called Peter and he was running late and I said it were be nice if you were come earlier but he came late and he didn't spend a lot time with me or his friend Ed and he pays Peter for the tickets and the foods was good, and then Peter hold my hand but he didn't introduce me until later has his girlfriend, and he wanted to go on the deck and suddenly I felt a little vertigo and a little while, Ed and I talked a while with Peter and then we said we need to go and Peter said why don't you comes over and Ed and said not today I need to go to work tomorrow and sees my dad.

So Peter gave me a kissed on lips and walks me to the van and then I got inside and Peter when to his car and then Ed got inside and we left and we headed back to Connecticut.

Also in June 1 is my nephew birthday and turn 25 year old.

When we got home from Mass and Ed talked me to the house and hold my hand because I felt a little vertigo when I got out of the car.

Then I said Ed when you gets home and give me a called and he did and also we called Barbie and said we didn't get lost and we just had to wait for the party but that was today and I told my mom and dad and about the party and also my brother and it was good foods and I am glad that I when to his party and met his friends, and they were very nice.

But time when by and so far I went to visit my boyfriend but he didn't comes to visit me yet, and I tell my friend Joe and he said don't you get mad at him and I said so far no but I were like to sees my boyfriend, more and not being selfish and I do invite him to comes over and I do need his company but I spent more time with Ricky, and Karen and Delores and Mark.

July 2010

Today was July 3 and today my dad and my brother and I went swimming and I dad swam a little bit and he wanted to watched the Yankees game and said the water was cold and said maybe I will go swimming on Sunday, and he watched the ballgame and tonight my brother said well we will not watched the movie today maybe on Sunday and on Sunday morning my dad said what are we going to have for lunch and Jean is only on the computer so I said soon I will finished and we will go stop and shop but my dad really wanted to go to Big Y but somehow we ended up at Stop and shop and we bought chunk steak but I thought it was rib steak and then fries and vegetable and then later that night we had hot dogs and my dad said they are really good and then he said well I have a stomach ache and I said we will take you to the hospital and asked twice and he refuse and said I am fine and he was sitting on his chair and then he tried to vomit, to make him feel better, and then after watching the Yankees, and my dad when to sleep and my brother was sleeping on the couch and he said good night to my dad went to sleep and got up about three times that night and the two times my mom heard him and then third time my mom fell asleep and then woke up and heard my dad bad snoring and thought that my dad was pretending, he likes to do that my mom tried to wake him up and but he didn't wake up and then she tried and tried so did my brother and then he woke me up and said something is wrong with dad, so I came downstairs and I tried to wake my dad get up and it was July 5, 2010, and Monday, and then I told my mom that I needed to called the ambulance to save my dad, and I got dressed and the ambulance arrival and they were working on my dad and then they took my dad into the ambulance and told us not to rush to the hospital and I called my sister and brother in law and told him what happened to my dad and he said he would tell my sister and later that day my sister and my brother in law was at the hospital and my nephew too and I also called Delores and told her about my dad and she couldn't believe it and then she came over and then my brother and I when to the hospital and later that day My mom and I and Delores when to sees my dad in ICU and at this time he was on life support and I was really upset and worry and I didn't wants my dad to died, but the doctor said that my dad had a massive stroke and he were never recover, and my mom asked if they can do something and the doctor and nurse said no.

The next day my friends Barbie and Ed took me and my mom to sees my dad and he was still under life support and I mom didn't want to let go of my dad because they were marry over 65 years together.

But soon they were going to cut his throat and then give my dad a feeding tube, and my sister explains that dad is in pain because of the life support tube and then in July 8, and around 2pm my mom said ok I will let the doctor to remove the tube and take him off life support.

They started to put some kind of medicine that he were not feel the pain and so the procedure started and about 4pm we when home because we saw that my mom couldn't handle it and seem like I couldn't neither and about two hours later, my father passed way, and the hospital called and my sister was there when my father died and now it was really hard to believe that my dad was gone so my sister called and asked if my brother wanted to sees dad and he said yes and my sister came to pick him up and when to the hospital.

My brother wanted to says goodbye to my dad when he passed away and so my sister pick up my brother and my mom and I am crying and I also called Peter about my dad passing and then I called my friend Barbie and Ed and friend Ricky, and I was crying and I couldn't believe that my dad was gone and he was never sick and he just died suddenly that was a shock to my mom and I and my brother, and my sister and brother in law.

Later that day my sister came with back from the hospital and now we had to arrange a funeral, and my sister said cremate or no cremate, so my mom was confuse that moment and she said no cremate, so then my mom said we don't have money I think that dad had life insurance, but he didn't, and now, my sister find the coffin and church and plot and then the stone will cost $15, 000.00 dollars and we don't we have the money but we were lucky that my sister did or otherwise the state would bury my dad, so now the funeral was set for Monday July 12, 2010 and now there is a problem, we need persons to carried the coffin to the church so I yes called Barbie and Ed and I told them when my dad funeral and Ed was coming and I told Ed that he will park his car and he will comes along with us, and then I called Henry and he said of course I will comes because I have a day off from work that day if I didn't I still would comes, and then I called my boyfriend Peter and I told him about the funeral and it will be on Monday and he said I will try to be there and I thought he were comes but I had a feeling that he were not comes, and ,meanwhile my mom was crying and saying I should have left him under life support and I was wrong if he was on life support I were sees him everyday and now he will be in the ground and I missed him so much.

Now at my house it felt strange because my dad was not around and now it only three of us and my brother and I were very close to my dad and we when places with my dad and now it going to be different, and it will never be the same, and I have talked with Barbie and Ed but I was crying.

Today is July 12, day of the funeral Ed came and parked his car and came inside and then about ten minute later, Karen came and I told them have a seat and then, about another ten minute later Henry came and now it was time to go to the funeral home and so Henry and I in one car and Karen follow us to the funeral home and my parents were left behind and Ed and Brother, and mom and Ed told how to get there and when I arrival, my sister came out of the funeral home and asked where are they? They are coming and soon and then my brother and mom and Ed arrival and when we step inside the coffin was open and my saw my dad lay in coffin and started to cry and my dad didn't looked the same and then we sat on the seat and then the man at the funeral spoke and alls our friends and my family said goodbye to my dad and now it was time to go to the Sacred heart Church for the mass and so the hearse and we follow the hearse and our car was the first one and then other cars follows and then we reach the church so they were not going use the step but the elevator and so my mom and I and my brother and the coffin went up first and then the rest follows.

The mass was about one hour and but I couldn't hear the priest and because he didn't speak clear and then a few friends of dad was there and then the mass was over and my dad had beautiful flowers and on the altar and then we alls started to leaves and my mom was crying so much and then she stop at the coffin and started to cried again and then I when up and I gave my mom a hug and then we headed out of the church and then we took the elevator and we headed to the "Sacred heart" Cemetery and there where my dad will lay in the coffin in the ground in the vault and the priest came and we place flowers on the coffin and my mom was crying so much, because she loved my dad so much and now he is gone.

We said goodbye and now we are headed to the restaurant and so we when to Angle at South Main street at that time I when with Karen and my mom and my brother and Ed when there and I met them a bit later.

So I make a wrong choice for a meal that was the worst chicken salads that I had in year but I ate some and so did my mom and Karen.

That day Karen left a little early because she had to go to work and we understood and then Ed and my mom and I and Henry we stay until the end and then Lucy talked with my sister and then we when home but it is not the same, but I thought that Peter would have comes and sees me but he said he couldn't handle it but didn't know that I really needed him to be there for me and I needed to hold someone that love me and care for me at that time.

But Peter did call me but that was not enough I needed him to be with me and to hold me and give me conform. But I am not being selfish but I needed him very much.

That day Henry came over and stay over for a while and then he had to go to the dentist and we thanks him for coming and being there here for the time of our loss and it was good seeing him and keep in touch and he said that he would.

I need to tell you how I felt when my dad passing away, at first I couldn't believe it but it did happened and he was a wonder dad and I will always remember my dad and he is in my heart and I do missed him a lot, and every days I wake up and thought it was a bad dream and but it was not and things will never be the same like before, our whole family will missed my dad.

Even our dog Susie does missed my dad my dog was use too lick his feet and now my dog is wander where is he? But I think that she known something happened to my dad and she is not a stupid dog.

About one week before my birthday Barbie called and said do you wants to go out to eat at first I hesitate and I not sure but then I went with Barbie and Ed and we when to "Great Taste" and I told them about my dad passing and then, I mention that my birthday is coming soon and before my birthday my sister took, us to Foxwoods and we played a little and but we were not happy and we won a little money and we had foods of course

I order hot dog with chill but I didn't think it were be so salty but it was, and my sister even tried it and she said I was right.

Later that night we when home but it didn't feel like home anyone more because my dad was not there, and I would not sees him again and that was really painful feeling to have, and I will never forget.

We went inside and my sister left and my mom went inside and started to cry again because she is missing my dad a lot, we are too.

Now it is July 31, Karen came over and we decided to take my mom to the Mohegan sun casino instead of I going to my reunion and so we when there and we played a little and then we when to lunch at PEPE Pizza at the casino and that day I treated Karen and my mom with my points and I order one pizza to go and I was happy and my brother wanted the pizza from there and the pizza that we ate at the casino, I gave Karen the leftover and because she took the time to take us there, and she is my dearest friend and I really care for her a lot and she is like my youngest sister and then we left the casino and Karen carry the large pizza and I was holding my mom and we were following Karen to the car and then we got to the car and Karen put the Pizza in the car and now we are alls in the car and now we are headed out of the garage and headed to 395 and now we are headed home and I send a text to my brother and he told that the mail came and then I said good and it took about one hour to get to the house and then went we got home, we alls when inside and Karen make the called and then I called Delores and Mark and Delores said that she was at the Millrace Bookstore and she asked me where would like to go for my birthday and I said Oliver garden and about five thirty, Delores and Mark came over and Pick me up and we left the house and we headed to Oliver garden and when we arrival I called my mom and Mark said I shouldn't called my mom that much and I know that he is right.

So we got out of the car and we went inside and our wait for about ten minute but we when into the bar section and sat at the booth and then they asked if we were going to order foods and Mark said yes we are and so they bought the menu and I order capnelli and so did Delores and Mark order lasagna and I order diet coke and we ate and then Mark surprise me and with a cake and candle and sang Happy Birthday and it was very nice of Delores and Mark, but one thing that my birthday was not the same because my dad is not here and I do miss him.

We alls do miss my dad and so feel that something is missing and so we are not the same anymore.

My dad was good and wonderful person that when through tough life but of most alls that he was a slave for the Germany and he work in the field and then he was taken to the camp that he ended up being about 70 lbs that he almost died and his farmer find him and if he didn't my dad probably were had died, but the farmer save my dad that came to America and work so hard and when holiday came, and we were not rich but we always had food on the table and pretty clothes on. I will never forget my dad and I will always love my dad and he was the only one that understood me and took my side and so I will really missed him so does my mom and my brother, especially my brother because they did the yard work together and they sometime argument but then they make up and then they when to the store and when I was not able too and my dad was very special and being with my mom over 64 years and they were very happy and sure they did fight but they didn't fight in any abuse but then they make up and they talk about the time when they were worker in Germany and how some of there friends got killed and they never when back to there family in Poland and my dad was born in Radom and had two brother and my dad written letter to them and then the letter stop and they don't know that he passed away, because they didn't have no contact address to reach them, so my mom told her niece about my dad and she loss two husband and they understood and so she spoke about my dad once on the phone, and she keep contact to with my mom and so we are trying ours best to deal the passing of my dad and sometime it is not easy. So I will change the topic, so now I will, talked about the big E. I have signed up to work at the Big E for September 18, 2010 and I took the shift from 10 am to 1 pm and I will be working in the Connecticut building and I am going with Barbie and Karen and I told Karen to comes at 645 am and we will be waiting for Barbie and I and Karen had cup of coffee and when Barbie came, she had to comes to the door because of Susie my dog were not let us go and I called out to my mom and brother to hold Susie and in my hand I had my poster and my tee shirt to give to the one that purchase my books. And also I will be seeing my boyfriend Peter and his friend Dante, and so when I was working, and I missed a called, the night before I was worry that I might have a episodes and I was really worry and I told Karen and Barbie at the Big E but that day I was fine and I met a lot of peoples and I passed out my tee shirt. Sold a lot of books and we when for lunch and I had Pizza and so did Karen and then we looked at Horses and cows and sheep and chickens that were coming out of the eggs and then we went to gate 9 to meet up with Paul and his friend Dante and then they came Dante when to the ATM to gets some cash and then Peter and Dante had pot roast and mash potatoes and then we walk and the parades when by Peter got me the necklaces that they were throwing and then I wear them and then we walks and walks and then Dante wanted to on his own and we suppose to meet up at the same location but it got change and we couldn't find him and then we did, because he was getting his picture of himself and then we waited and waited and then we when to the concert and then we listen to Paul Reverse and Raider, and the song was Louie, and Peter and sang the song and now we were walking them to gate 9 to make sure that they were not get lost, then Peter gave me a kissed and we walks back but we make a few time. That day Barbie was corn on the cob and on the stick and some vegetables and share with Karen at that time I was doing my book event.

But I did called my mom we would be coming home soon but we came home late but that was ok with my mom, because my doesn't know how to communication with my brother with the sign language, and it is difficult for her, and when I came home Karen left and when home and our feet were really hurting that day, and then I got in and I took my pill and I change and I had a pizza grinder for dinner because I was hungry.

But I was glad that I saw Delores and Mark, and I do miss my friends they are working at the Big E and they will be finishing up on October 3, 2010 and I wander how I did with my sales of my books.

Two days ago I saw my friend Ricky and we went to Open house about skiing and boating and there was good foods and I do enjoy his company but I do missed my boyfriend very much and I hope to sees him soon, Barbie and I and Karen will plan to go to Worcester and then we talked and go out to eat and maybe watch a Movie.

But I don't know went it going too happened but I will asked Barbie, when she has day off on Saturday, and that day I will sees my boyfriend Peter.

Today is October 1, and it is Friday and we are having a storm Nicole and the power was off for three hours and it came on and I was worry that we might not have lunch if the power off and then about three hour later the light when on and I was happy and then I make chicken pie for me and my mom but I am very worry about my mom because she think of my dad a lot every morning I think of my dad and how he got up and had coffee and looked at the Hartford section at looked at the Yankees rating and then he really liked watching the game every night that they were playing and then we watched a lot movie and my brother and my dad like watching war movie but my mom and I didn't.

Ok talked about boyfriends, Gary was different from Peter, and Gary wanted to spend a lot time with me and he wanted to be around me almost every day and we had breakfast and we did things together and sure sometime he did hurt me and I cried but he wanted to be around me a lot and I was happy about that I also spend time with his children and he really loved me and so we when places and I was included about Peter seems like he just want to leave me behind and back to Gary he visit and we took walks around the block and his son Nick and Catherine stay with my parents and so we were a family and it was good between Gary and I and I also enjoy his company, and I don't understand that why that Peter doesn't want to be here when I need him the most and my father passed away and I cannot understand why? He said that he loved me but why he is not here? I need him to hold me and tell me that everything will be all right, I just need the support and love that I need so much from him. He is not the around and it does hurt my feeling and I do really, really, do need him and where is he? Well he is never around when you need him. But it was not really fine with me but I said it was. So far it is two or three days and he have not called me if I am all right! Yes I am worry but he make me a little stress and I don't like that, and my friend Ricky were come over if I invited him everyday but he is only a friend, and I do need to go out with my friends like Karen and Ricky and Barbie and Ed, but I really need to sees my boyfriend and he were should take me out and let me have some fun and forget for while and have less stress in the house and then I do miss my friend Delores and Mark and but they are working at the Big E and I will be seeing my friends and I miss talking to them and I wander how I am doing with my books and I hope I sell more than last year and my dad were be proud of me but I know that he is seeing everything, what a I am doing and but back to my boyfriend, I thought he were be here for me and but not here for me when I needed his support and I really need him to be here and I think that he doesn't understand what I need and I am not being selfish and but seem, like he called his friend in New Haven and leave me waiting for that called but sometime he talked non sense and I really don't like it, but his friend in New Haven she talked about her dad and about her problem and she tell me about Peter and how he lived in New Haven and sometime has panic attack and called the ambulance and took him to the hospital and my boyfriend like to move around a lot, but it were be nice if he move back to Connecticut and we can be together and not being alone and sometime don't hear from him but those email, I feel that I wants more out of life, and also life is to short and you should be with someone that loved you and you don't know what tomorrow will bring, and so back to my dad, every morning I wake up and I think that I would sees him and that was only a nightmare, but it is not and I will sees my dad again and talked to him again, the last time I spoke to my dad was July 4, 2010 on Sunday, and he was fine and on the next day my mom tried to wake my dad and my mom was unable and my brother and I and we couldn't wake him and we called 911 and they came and they work on my dad and they couldn't wake him up and then they took my dad to New Britain General and we when to the hospital and they put my dad on life support and my mom asked can you do anything for him and the doctor said sorry, your husband had a massive stroke and he will not recover and my mom refuse to listen to the doctor and my dad continue to be life support and my dad not getting better, but it is hopeless and my dad is going to died and we go back and forward to the hospital and my dad is lay on the bed on the bed like a vegetable and I believe my mom need to let him go but she is not ready, and so my dad died three days later and on the day that my dad died, in the car I heard the life support machine that was the air condition and it was making that weird sound and it really scare me, and then my air condition in my room make that sound too and it really scare me again and one night I saw a floating globe in the hallway and I didn't says to anyone and on the walls I sees my dad, so don't called me crazy, I believe we are a very close family and so that why I am seeing my dad and I know that my mom talked about my dad a lot and it is hard for my mom because they were together for over 64 years and with the good and bad and I know that they loved each other and my mom having hard time dealing with the death of my dad, but life goes and I don't know how my mom will deal with the holiday and one thing I know it is not same.

It does not seem that same thing right now, on October 8, 2010, is three month and I hope that I am repeating myself but my dad was good and we when to church and we when everywhere and he really enjoy watching the Yankees, and red sox games and he looked in the newspaper how they were doing and would they make it too the world series and then it they lost the game, he blame the manager or the pitcher and then he like also watching the war movie and telling us how when he was working for the Germany and how he survive the war and he how he came to American and it was not easy but my dad was a hard worker and he worked over 35 year at the factory at FAFNIR Bearing Company and my dad retired in 1986 went he was 64 and half year old and my dad also work part time for

J C Penney for 1 day and then my dad work at sears and for a long time and then they laid him off and he got stock and sold it and stay home and work in his garden and he really like that very much, and about family in Radom Poland, probably gone too and no contact over 20 years and so, about my mom has a niece and she still lives in Poland and she called my mom once in a while and we also send her package to her and she has two sons and one daughter and they lives near Warsaw and my mom is not that strong and she had chill yesterday and hope that she is fine, so back to holiday and well my dad at thanksgiving we when to my sister house and I am not sure if we are going this year, and back to my dad the funeral was a fortune and my dad didn't have prepaid and it was a lot of money, and the money that we didn't have.

I am sure that my dad did help out with the American Soldier in 1945 with working bulldozer and he was freed from the Germans, and he met my mom and they were wed, and they came to American and with my sister and then my brother was born and then two year I was born and then I was a really sick child that almost died and it was not once but twice, or third times.

Yes peoples making fun of me and peoples thought that something was wrong with me like I was a retard but I can says that I was slow but I was still normal, and I am normal and I do drive a car and I take care of my money and sure I did have money trouble, so I am not the only one.

Now back to Gary, on November 14, it will be his birthday and I just want to wish him a happy birthday and he is in my heart always. He really treated me well and we got along and he really like my parents and especially he called my mom grandma, and my mom didn't get mad about that, and most of alls I will have Gary and my Dad always in my heart and I will never forget them, never, now I do love my boyfriend Peter and I wish that he were spent more time with me, and hope to sees him soon and hope that he were called me soon, and I am still dealing with my dad and I still cannot believe it but I must go into reality and understand that he is gone and my dad will not come back home again and he is in a better place, and we do miss him very much. What I learned in the newspaper I would took my dad to the hospital and he were probably alive but I didn't know the signed of the stroke and the high pressure, that were give my dad a massive stroke, but now it is too late and he is gone and I wish that I told my brother to take my father to the hospital on July 4, and they probably were give my dad some kind of medicine and then he were be with us and now I blame myself I wish that I helped my dad but we thought he was fine and we didn't know the symptoms of the stroke, and I should have looked it up or just took him to the hospital but I didn't and then before my dad went to sleep and I thought to myself hope nothing else worst wouldn't happen but you know it did and my dad had the massive stroke and he died after we remove from life support, but how were I know that he were died the next day and he was fine and we asked him and he said he was ok.

I think that I am repeating myself so I will let it go and my dad is in a better place now and I will really missed him and so does my mom and my brother and my dog" SUSIE" and we just have to move on and live without my dad and I know it is difficult but it will be fine and the holiday will never be the same. Halloween is coming and so far we didn't get any candies for the kids so far but we will and then Thanksgiving November 2010 without my dad and I think that Peter will be coming over and I do want to sees my boyfriend more than less, so about couple month ago my boyfriend asked me to move in but somehow it is not the right timing because there is always something happened and so seem like it does not works out but maybe I don't suppose to live with Peter but just being with him.

Last night I spoke with Peter and he has some guy over Joe with him and I think Peter has some kind of company but he does miss me and I do miss him, and the weather is rainy and cold and now it is fall and the leaves are changing colors and then so far my dad didn't get a gravestone because of the weather.

About Jean Marie, well my thought are still about my dad and my mom is crying a lot and I cannot deal with the a lot of crying and it really hurting and I cannot explains how I feel I think that I feel numb and I do not know how to handle the loss and how I should feel, but I do not understand why my dad passed way and he was not sick and he was healthy and suddenly he was gone and today is five month October 5, 2010 and my dad in the coffin and in the grave in the ground and we cannot sees him or speak to him again and that the hard part of living without my dad and sometime I didn't wanted to be means but I just was a bit mean and I hope that he understand that I loved him very much and I missed him very much.

Every time when I go into the bedroom I think that my dad there but he is not and so it is difficult times but it is much harder for my mom and my brother because my dad and my brother work together and they walks around the yard, and dig garden and pick the leaves and putting into the bag and then in the barrel, and then put into trash.

Then they discuss about fencing, and then I called and hasting fencing and they order the fence, my dad and my brother, agree to purchase on May 2010. But we waited and waited but the fence came after my dad death and my dad missed out.

Then my dad and brother decided to buy a step for the front and they are very nice.

Talked about the garden, my brother growth a watermelon and two big one, and a lot tomatoes and a lot peppers, from our garden and they grew so big.

I am the only I can do know to do sign language, but my mom does not know how to do it and my sister does not know how.

I need to says I am scared of dying and I have fear and I don't want to know when it happened, I should says I am terrify about talking about this topic, I am really scares, I do not know how handle this. I know that you are born and I thought you live forever, but you don't but reality hit you and you will not live forever, so if it happened how do you handle it, I really do not want died, but you no matter, that day will comes will you be ready, but one thing when you know when that day comes, god don't let me know, I want died in my sleep, but not yet! I need to help my mom and help her with mom medicine and make sure that she is fine….

I believe that everyday of your life you should be with the peoples that you love and care, be happy and be positive and not be sad and if you loss someone you loved your dad or your boyfriend that passed away in 2003.

Gary who died in 2003, but died from a massive attack, and he was a wonderful man, and kind person, just like my dad.

Well talking about " death" let talked about life, each day if you like dancing go dancing and be with your friends.

Just don't sit home and soaked, that is a bad ideas, so get up and called your friends, you don't know if you are going to see you again.

Do enjoy your life, life is too short, so go out and have fun go the movie or go to the beach, or even going to the casino.

If you like go to the casino, and go to the concert, if you music like the moody blue, or beach boys. So go for it…

Don't hold back, just go out and have fun, sees your boyfriend, or friends, go to a Yankees game or rolling skating.

If you like to read, so pick up a book and read it, and so if you like to listen to lady gaga, the best thing is sometime to meditation.

But I loved dancing but ever since the vertigo, but vertigo affect my life since I had it and I cannot get rid of vertigo, but I still living with vertigo and I cannot drive the car, and I feel like a handicap, but I am not.

But I cannot wait when I am well again, and then I cannot wait to drive myself to the store and to the doctor, I just want to well and I want to be normal, I know I will be soon. I know I will be.

Broadcasting

Well I went broadcasting school and I did graduation and that time I went to a TV workshop with Neal. It was television network, and edited and it was fun, and then I was invited to the mixer…

But I attended every week to Farmington to the school and then to his house, and he was very nice, then I went to his house and I used his computer and edited some stuff, and added some music and then some other students would there too.

Also went to the Newington studio doing some taping and a lot comedy and I was watching them taping and on the cue, and then we took a break and then about half hour we did more taping, and we when to Wendy and had a great lunch and after lunch, we discuss what will happened next.

Then it was at rocky hills at a other studio and more comedy and brother drove me that Sunday at first we couldn't find the place and my brother was angry, but then he was fine, and once time Barbie went to a mixer during the summer, and we had hot dogs and hamburger.

But we didn't stay wait a movie, because she wanted to leave and I had no choice but I wanted to stay longer.

One time Ricky went to the mixer to the Newington, and Ricky I met my friends, and I passed out my business cards and I had good foods.

Later that night, Ricky and I went to Chicopee to a dance, and we stay there until 1 am. Then we danced to the music, and Ricky, had beers and I had water, and after the we left and headed home and I was happy, but he stay for awhile and then he when home that night, and we talked for a long while and he gave me a hug and then he gave me a kiss when he left.

Went we got home and went inside and talked, about two hour he left.

I used go to studio times but that was good and I ran into to Neil one of teacher, he said hello.

Then I went too talked to Kevin about getting a job, and I went to nutmeg TV. And met a man name Ryan for the intern about the job, but I didn't get the job, but my dream job would be TIC 96.5 and I would like be a music department, and promotions, I would to work there that is my dream, do what I loved. That is my dreams, and I hope to god, that would make me very happy, but that is dreams, but will it happened? I don't know, but I hope so but time will tells and so I need to have things to do studio time before I got the vertigo and then driving the car and then going places but somehow I am being stops because of my vertigo and then I don't know, seem like I just stop living, but I am alive and I want to do what I did before I got the vertigo and I drove to school everyday and never miss day and I got there early and then I got a good grade and then I graduation, and now I just need to find a job and it is over three year and it is angry and stressful not having a job and I think that one day I will get a job that I loved to do.

I believe that I did much better on radio and not TV because on TV you needed to know the about the timing but with radio, the commercial and the song and some songs are different and you need a counter between the song and you must give the station letter to let the listener to know and then you need to entertain the listener and you need to be popular and I think that is a great job being radio personally and you do your things and then you meet celebrity like Carrie Underwood and then Lady GAGA and you go out there to interview them, and I think that is awesome and also a lot of work, and seem like it is exciting, about being on the radio, and about the peoples on TV and you are in the spotlight, just like the news peoples and that is great.

That is my dreams job but beside that I would not making a movie and I probably would make a comedy, but I know that I need to do something big and getting notice, but I need to get notice I don't have a clue how to make it and put it together, so I am thinking loud whatever I do I need to do extra hard, I feel if I did something big, I am not sure what kind of reaction I would get, but I understand why peoples think that something is wrong with me but it is not, and I am normal just like you and I am not different, I am just you maybe a bit older or the case younger.

But I like something with my experience, to do what I know and accomplished my dreams and am someone and have a mark that I did something with my life.

Not just sitting back not doing nothing I believe I need to do that because if I don't if I don't success, I feel I don't want to fail and I don't want to be negative, but I want be positive and get the job, that I went to school and before that I need to brush up on my training, and go to the studio and practice and practice and I am not give up so I am going to do it.

Yes, I am not going to wait for too happen I am going out and search that dream, besides writing and I need to be in the media. Before my parents hold me back now, I probably would be on my own but now I will never know. But now no one is holding me back, but myself, one thing that I need to get ahead and have a paycheck, of course I get royalty for my books but I am not famous but everyday I do struggle whatever I do, also I don't too repeat myself, I always had thing about being in the media, ever since junior high, there was a time that I wanted to be a singer, and than a actress went I got out of high school, and my parents would against my dream, and now if I never find out, but that was a big mistake. I just listens to them and I did not follows my dreams, because I got the guilt from my parents and I was adult and I was afraid to sees if I would make it New York, I feel that I did fail myself, maybe I would be someone and not unknown, but I didn't I just gave up on myself and I blame my parents and myself, not standing up for myself…

Dreams

What dreams for Jean Marie, well being on Connecticut style and better Connecticut that is my dreams and also being interviews " Good Morning" and I would like hit all the circuits, and I would tell them how I became a author, but it was not smooth sailing, and how my dreams became reality, but also being myself, and I know I do have story to tells, well you saying that I want too be notice, and make a better life for myself and for my mom and brother and not wandering how will I pays my bills, or I have enough money, that were make very happy and I know that my dad is watching us. If you do have dreams, and you should go after them and not giving up on them, go for it and you will not be sorry like I am. That I didn't follow.

Only if I did my life were been totally different but I didn't do anything about my dreams but I just let then runs my life, and now I know it was a mistake but if I had to change it I would and maybe I would be more on my own and not being like a child and but a grown up and not like a child.

About having a dreams that could be impossible but you need to believe in what you are doing and what you wants out of life, and so you don't forgive up but you should go after that dreams and never, never, never give up what you wants out of life.

You know that dreams do comes true. And went you really work hard what you wants and go for it and you will not regret, and you don't, then you will regret, so put your foot in front and says yes I will make my dreams comes true, whatever you want to be a writer, artist, actors, or singers, so for it and don't let your parents or your boyfriend tamper your dreams.

The only one will be successful will be you and I believe that if I didn't write my first book, I were never became published author.

Sure, even though I didn't go through regular channel, but when through self published, sometime, I think I didn't make alls the money that I spend to do self publish, but one thing I believe in me so I just had write this book, and my first book was "Father and Sons Hobby" and this book is about my boyfriend and I and his children and his hobby shop,, so I believe that was the only ways to remember him by writing this book and I am glad that I did.

Then I accomplish the second book " No Ending Dreams" and then my other dreams was that I got interview by Hartford Courant, and the New Britain Herald, and also been on Cable TV and had a interview and that was awesome but I was very nervous on the show but my dreams did comes true.

I was very happy and exciting about being in the Newspaper and Cable TV.

Men in life

So how should say about men in my life, so I mean boyfriends, well some men that I know that what just wants to be friends, so that is nothing wrong.

In my case I sees more of my friends than I sees my boyfriend and I don't understand and I am not complaining, but it were be nice to sees him once in a while and he were comes and visit me, I guess you know who I am talking about right now, Peter. But it is really difficult for that man to comes over and he make a lot of lame excuses and sometime I don't even believe him but I should and trust him but I don't because comes up too many stories and it is hard to believe him and my friend Ricky wants to spend a whole a lot time with me but I am not cheating on my boyfriend but he is a good friend and care about me. Two men in my life are totally different because my friend want to spend a lot of times with me but my boyfriend is always busy and doesn't have time for me when I need him the most, and when my father passed way and I needed my boyfriend too be with me but he was not.

He said that he couldn't handle it but he should been here for me.

But I have another friend and I never met him but he was there for me and he understood me and his name is Joe and he once lived in New York but now he lived in Florida and when I am upset and he is for me and vice verse and my boyfriend has friends that lives in New Haven and I talked with and she tell me about Peter because he is self centered person, and he doesn't care about anyone but himself and if you want to says something he cut you off and said I am busy now and hang up the Phone and his friend told me that she doesn't wants him to hurt me and I know what kind of man that I am dealing with, but I am scare of him and he is that ways and I am not making excuses for him but he should give me a called and sees how I am doing and so, but I am not going to called him so I am going to wait for his calls.

Well, my boyfriend, Peter was nice when I met him about four year ago and we went to the movie and even to California Pizza when I had a little cold and it was really drafty and so we waited for the table and then we sat down at the table and of course I wanted a pizza, and sometime I could go for chicken finger and those my favorite foods, and probably a cheap date too.

But I went out with Ricky and we when Robin Burger and he had the biggest burger and I had chill of course but it was too hot and I left it and Ricky took and said not too hot and then I left it and we pays separate check and then we headed to the movie but I don't remember which movie that we went too.

Later that night, after the movie Ricky decided to take me dancing to Chicopee and it was fun and I met some of his friend and then we dance and then it was time to leave and we walks to the parking lot and headed to Connecticut and then we got home and my dad and my mom was there and then we sat in the kitchen, and we played a card game and then Ricky was not in the mood and so he said I got to get up and said bye and then went he got home he gave me a called and but my boyfriend should understand, that I am not cheating him but just being with my friend. Ok back to Joe and Karen and I will meet that man sometime in the future, but the both times that we suppose to meet him, he just cancel out and then we didn't arrange anymore with Joe, unless he comes to Connecticut or we go to Florida, but I don't think so, not now because we cannot afford it.

But one day Karen and I will meet my friend Joe and Karen I will have a vacation but I believe not this year because our money is tight and we are probably will go to Pennsylvania and it is much better and the trip will be in 2011 and I think that I could afford but flying to Florida and that is a bit too much money and I really cannot afford it and I do like going to Pennsylvania and it is like old country and peaceful, and seeing Joe that will be at a later date and meanwhile I will be texts him and talking to him and he is a good friend and back to my boyfriend Peter, he does not have time for me and I really don't know what he is doing and but never have time for me and I am feeling alone and lonely without him and I wish that he were comes and visit me but one thing about him he wants me to visit him and I don't understand but he just hang out with his friend in Worcester and he does not comes to Connecticut since his mom move to Pennsylvania and he used to go Orange and west haven and now he does not comes to New Britain, and when my dad passed way he did not shown up and that day I needed him the most and I tried to understand if he needed me I were be there for him and one thing he is totally different from the men that I date.

It were be great that he were comes and sees me and we do things that were really help me and I would feel better and I have to handle things on my self and I thought when someone love you they should be there for you and stand by you and hold and says that everything will be ok! But he is with his friend and I am forgotten by him and sometime he hurt me and apology a lot so I believe that he should not hurt me but just love me and has I love him and don't asked me nonsense questions and stupid and I don't them and so I don't know how to tell him but being rude and means to me that is totally wrong about that. Sometime he does get on your nerve, but you tried not to get upset and tried not to cried neither, so if you do he win and you lose.

Yes I am getting a bit tired when he is with his friends he doesn't called me and I do get upset and he does hurt me that ways.

But I also don't wants to repeat myself and I just want to be happy and not too complain and be with the one that you love and his name is Peter.

But he was very nice when I met him but he changed afterward.

Love of my life

So he was mister nice guy when I met him and he was very friendly and comes over and then there was an incident that he didn't show up and didn't even gave me a called and at that time he didn't have a cell phone.

The next day he apology and so many times and times, until I forgave him but his pattern doesn't change, he think that he get way with it but sometime he does and I really don't like it and I don't like his behaving and his matter,, seems like sometimes that he does not have them and well about his personality, mister nice guy and when he is upset he is just totally a person that you don't want to speak too, because he is so means and he yelled and said I am mad at you and it is not even your fault but he likes to blame someone else beside himself, and he make plans and then he make up a lot excuses and then he said well I cannot make it and I was in the emergency room or runaway to Maine to his friend, and stay there, and especially when you need him and he is not around, I don't understand about that's!

Sometime when you need him to be around and he is not around and he doesn't even called you if he does he is dealing with his problem and his friends and sometime included to a limited, but not much and sometime he does not says bye and he just hang up and that really, really hurt me and I don't like that's! but Peter does not have peoples manner but he does not know how to deal with someone that has a loving family, well he told me something that he remember last year about " Thanksgiving" and about my dad having a drink and the " Smile of his face" you still could picture it today and you will never forget that.

Ands we are not going to sees that smile again, because he is gone and

I will says much about dad now but I do missed him very much and he was good to me and my mom and brother and sister and my nephews.

But back to my boyfriend, well he does comes over and he stayed and then he leave and he does not tell you where he goes and he is very secret about the where about and then when he get home like early morning and then he called you and wake you up sometime it is good but then you are unable to go back to sleep.

Later that day Peter called me and asked when will I comes to Worcester and cook for him and I said well you know that I am not a highway driver and then last night he asked me am I happy at that point I was not sure how I was happy or a little sad, I really didn't have a answered but I did not says anything at that time and then he said I got to go and then he hung up and I have not heard from him yet! But I know that I will and so I am not worry and soon I will be visiting him with Karen and Barbie and Ed and we are going to sees Peter and Dante.

So that will be happening on November 20, 2010 and that is couple day before Thanksgiving, and I am really excited, and now back to his personality and it is not the nicest but he is my boyfriend and we are together for four year plus and we do gets along and my friends says that I deserve someone better than he is., but he is fine and I don't listen and also his friend from New Haven she gets a lot time mad at him for not talking enough and cutting it short and then there are other stuff too, that really gets her mad and so far he did not to that too me so far that I don't remember.

Today I find out that my boyfriend went to the hospital, and when to the ER and think that his eye had a vessel burst in his eye but I hope that he is ok.

But I receive an email from Peter and told me about his eye and I am worry about him and I hope that he will give me a called.

But I know that Peter will be coming for Thanksgiving and will be with my family and it will not be the same.

On the day of thanksgiving, hope that Peter will be on time, and we have a nice times at my sister house and we were a family together, that day!

So let me tell you how Peter looked like, well he is tall, and mean that he is taller than I and he has black hair and a little bald on top and he and on the medium size and then he wear glasses when he drive the car. But sometime his manner stink and he can be nice too me but sometime he is very rude and means to me and make me cried.

But he also likes to go to many colleges and he gets his degree and he is smart on something and stupid on others.

But I am not calling him stupid because I am not that smart enough and then no one is smart, he should not be defense.

Peter and I like the same kind of music and foods and then but one thing that I am catholic but I am not going into religion.

Says if Peter is Jewish but we are on the same page and we do get along and that alls that should matter and I think that you should agree what I say.

Religion and faith should not inference and then love shouldn't matter and you should support the one that you love and if he wants you to live with him and you should.

No one should not stop you, and you should know, love has a lot do with the one that you love and you should not be control by anyone you should be the only person that should make the decision in your life and if you want to be home or if you want to be with your boyfriend, no one should not stop you because you should make your own mistakes.

Because you will learn from them and you should be a better person and your love will be stronger, so you're a big girl so acted like one.

So get into your car and drive to Worcester and sees him and tell him that you want him and make love to him and you will be the happier girl.

Who is Jean Marie?

Well I have many sides of myself, well I have the good side and I am friendly and kind and I am also a girl had her feeling hurt my peoples in my own family and in my own family my brother and dad and even my sister make fun of me and I don't know why? Do I have a sign on my face saying that I am pathetic I don't know a clue, but one thing I am the only one that can communication with my brother and he is deaf and my mom and dad and sister and but my mom has difficult to talks with my brother, and I am not in ashamed that my mom when to school for awhile and then my grandmother make her work on the farm and I believe that was not right and when there were times that I taught my mom but later on she refuse to learned and I stop.

Because my mom got really upset and said I cannot do this and leaves me alone so I gave her the respect and I left her alone, but then my dad yelled at my mom and said don t you want to learned and my mom said no and my dad said it were be good for you and my mom said leave me alone and that was the end of it and no more discussing about learning about writing or reading so, when we go to the restaurant and I tell my mom what on the menu, and I order what I am having and at the restaurant my mom use the excuse that she forgot her glasses, but I am proud of my mom because she raise us good and she is a good mom and a good cook and then she is also smart even that she didn't go to school., and then the German took her from her home and work for the Germans and she had a tough life and it was not easy because my mom didn't sees my grandmother and since that she was fourteen year old then after that my mom came to American and never since did not sees her mom again.

But after the war, my grandmother when to red cross and search for my mom and they found each other and they written letter, and about fifteen year old my grandmother passed way and it was very sad and but we never knew her. But then about five year my mom niece keeps contact with my mom and our family and her name is DANUTA, and that is Diane in English.

Ok back to me, well everyone has a good side and back I mention that all ready, well I do get very angry and I like to bang the door or yelled and screams but that is when I really get angry and I tried to control it and it is easy but sometime it is difficult with short fuse and it blow up and you don't want to hurt anyone but you do, and then you feel sorry and but it is too late.

I believe that everyone do not understand me, and I do gets along with my family and friends but there are times that sometime that the fuse just goes off and you have no control of it. And I don't understand that why I gets mad at the peoples that I love and care for.

Before my dad death, I got really angry and I yelled at him and said that he didn't know how to drive the car and he said I should be driving and I believe that he was right, and I am lucky that we didn't have accident that day I probably could been dead too, but my dad didn't died of automobile accident, but a massive stroke and in some ways my mom was right that maybe we should have took my dad to the hospital and probably he would be alive today, if they check his blood pressure and did the MRI and now it is too late, and I do feel guilty I should have not listen to my dad and called the ambulance on July 4, and I don't have it were have turned out.

But I cannot swell on it so I need to let him go and I let him lay in peace.

I do not know why I am feeling that ways but I do being myself since the flu shot and I have a lot of headache and then I feel tired and seems like something wrong with me, well on October 16, 2010 I when to the CAPA meeting I was fine, and I was happy that I when with Mark and Delores and then, after the meeting I thought that I was going home but we didn't so we when for lunch at Wood and tap and I was fine going inside the restaurant and order chicken tender and fries and then we stay and talked while with Don and Ruth and but seem like they were making fun of me.

Also I think that Delores and Mark did too and I felt a little down and I didn't says much, and I was quiet and Don and Ruth said well Jean Marie, will have a lot material for her book, I should in a quote.

We stay for awhile and we pays the check and then we left the restaurant and then headed to the car but Mark was in the restroom and then a little ways down to the car something weird happen to me, suddenly I fell on my right leg and I saw them looking at me and then I felt a faint and then I felt hot and I was really scare and I don't think so that I lost my footing and before I felt I had a bad feeling that something was going to happen and I only knew what I would have hold on to the car and probably I were not fall, and Delores and Mark, but especially Delores asked if she should take me to the hospital, and they walks me to the car and I when into the back seat and suddenly my ears got block and then they got into the car and now we were headed home and now I am seeing white all the ways home and I was terrify what was happening, and then went we got to my exit I got better but my leg was still in pain, and then we got into my driveway and then the car was in Park and Delores walks me to the house and Susie was barking her hat off and then Delores, then left me at the door and my mom came and said what happen and I couldn't explain and after that's I put ice on the leg and then I change into my night clothes and I just seat there and wander what happen to me and I cannot figure it out and so it was like a mystery to solve and I was the object and lately I have a lot of headache and blurr vision and my eyes are giving me a problem too, but I still think it has something with the flu shot and ever since I am not feeling well.

But the night of the injury it was very difficult to go to the bed and to climb the bed and then I just figure out not too have pain and so I when on the bed a different ways and it was much better.

So on October 16, I when early to the meeting because Delores and Mark pick me up and I find out that I am getting money for my two books but I think that they should check it out and I think it was three and the book title was Night of Terror and I think that they probably sold it and just forgot to added on and but also there was a lot crowds and they were coming into the booth and maybe even stealing but I don't know and I don't want to accuse anyone if I don't have proof and I don't wants to says that my fan wanted to have my book free and at this point I don't know what happen.

Well, yesterday I suppose to go with Barbie to the health fair but after I fell I cancel out because I was scare, and I really could walks, and so I stay home and my brother make such a good chicken on the grill and said my dad probably were like it but it taste like outback but even better and we had shell and vegetable and it was a good lunch and then we had left over polish lasagna, and it beef with rice and coleslaw and cook in the oven that my sister make and it is delicious and my brother really like it very much.

But ever since the fall I thought did I get dizzy and but I didn't, so what really happen, my conclusion is that I just miss the step and then I fell but before I did I seen it in my eyes and that was like a premonition and I think it is and the same thing happen, night before my dad when to sleep and I thought to myself hope that my dad will be ok, and then it was not.

So am I physicking? I don't know.

Sometime I cannot explain thing that I know and I think but I don't know want to know the future, but I just want to live one day at the time, and I know that I need to control my weight and lose weight and maybe I have a balance problem, but one thing I do not have high blood pressure, and my sugar I don't know, and I hope not then I will be like my mom and I don't want to have the same problem like my mom or dad and I do want to be healthy and so I pray to god that I don't have any problem in the future, but I guess I told about the vertigo, and that is like running my life and I hope to god to be normal and that I were be able to drive and go to the store and help out my brother but I notice that every day I have like a block in my ear since the flu shot and I hope that the doctor didn't give a effect one, and I don't want to get sick because my mom is counting on me to help her.

Thinking Positive

Well, how ever you feel and you down, I believe that you should feel positive and you should not let thing get you down.

I feel that Peter like too put me down sometime and like that I don't have enough intelligence but I do and I also know how to cook and well he has panic disorder and he just somehow manage to go the hospital and taking pills but in my case I did have a panic order and but I am not taking any pills and I am fine and I can deal with the good and the bad so I think that I am much stronger than Peter and I can do things and I do get things accomplish.

But he put me into the negative because he think that I am not smart enough but I know that I am and sometime I think that some peoples talked behind my back and even the peoples that they are my friends. I feel that they treated me different and I am a normal person just like them.

Well on the positive note, I don't care what they think but I did write 24 book and now this my 25th book and it is alls about me and my family and so, a lot peoples asked how can you put alls this into a book? Well the secret is that if you have a story so why don't you tell it and then you will end up being a publish author but you will be a local author unless the New York times or being on the "Good Morning America" then you hit national and if your really lucky and get on OparanWinfery show, then your really lucky and you hit the jackpot and you are on the bestseller. But that is one in a million shot, and I am not really lucky.

But I need to stay in the positive attitude and whatever you do you should have a positive, and well some peoples are proud of me but some don't even asked how I am doing with my books, well that is my sister and my brother in law and even my two nephews, and my dad was proud of me and so is my mom but not my brother.

But I still keeps on writing because I do enjoy this and I don't know if this is my best work but I know like that my fan would know who I am and I have nothing to hide and I am open honest person and I were not steal if I were be homeless, because I believe it is dishonest and just be truthful and one more things you should be honest with everyone and have no secret, but now I might sound like a phony but I am not.

I am just trying to be positive like you or me, but it were be a better world and the peoples that you love were not hurt you but in some ways they do because they don't have time to talked with you and your boyfriend is helping young guys finding them home but I believe they are capable to do on there own and so on the positive note two, sure if I did decided to move in with Peter I would tell him that no I don't wants these boys here and I would leaves,, I don't know them, and they might hurt me.

Moving in with my boyfriend

Yes my boyfriend asked me to move in but he is sometime not a nice person and does hurt my feeling and then he thinks that I were pays for his foods and then for gas, and he think that I am rich, even though that I am not rich and I don't believe that I should treated him for dinner and then for gas, at this point I feel that he is using me, and he said that he loved me, I believe if someone loved you they don't asked for money and said, I am really poor and I cannot afford foods, but the others side of my boyfriend Peter, well his friend from Maine called him ands said why don't you come and visit him and so Peter pack up his bags and headed to Maine and stay there for a weeks, and meanwhile he doesn't called me, and I am not sure if he is ok or not and he avoid to tell me things and it is like a big secret, some of my friends told me to just let him go and find someone else.

But I do love him in someway but not when he is rude and means and make me cried, and hurt my feeling and sometime stand me up and that really hurt me and think that I am dumb or something but I know that I am not.

I think I know I haven't move in with Peter, because he always wants his ways and everything that he says right and what you says is not correct.

Also Peter said that he is not coming to Connecticut, because he were get less money I really don't understand that's!

But I am not going there and but I need to says that Peter are dating over four years, and we are happy, ands we are survive the long distance relationship and when he, live in West Haven, I had to take the train and visit him and I visit him more than he did, and that is unfair, or asked my friend Karen or Barbie to take me to Peter.

Sure I had other boyfriend in the past they took time to visit me and

I visit them, and I don't understand about Peter, because he is totally different from the men that I had in the past.

But we do get along and he asked me nonsense questions that it really gets me mad and I don't like what he says sometime.

One Saturday, that he couldn't reach me so he called my friend Karen, and I think that was a lame excuse to speak to her, but my phone was working and I think that he didn't tried to called me just called her instead, well I am trying to says that was only a excuse, and he was not that worry if he was he were try and tried again but he just called Karen and said that he was worry and he couldn't reach me and that was a lies.

About moving in with Peter, is not the right time, because who were watch my mom and who were take care of her, well my brother does not communication well with my mom and that were not work, and I asked Peter too come over and stay overnight and he still didn't visit me.

When I needed him the most he was not around and said that he couldn't handle it and about me when I needed someone to hold me and tells me that I were be ok, no still Peter didn't show up yet, so the last time I seen him at the Big E with his friends and mind.

Also Peter asked if we wanted to visit him but we told him that we cannot at this time so, his friend Dante, asked us to visit him in Worcester, and so we have plan to visit my boyfriend on November 20, with Barbie and Karen and I and Ed I think so if he is not working and we alls are going to sees Dante and Peter, well I will sees how this will be and I hope that Peter will be nice but not rude, but Barbie and Peter don't really gets along and I hope that I will not cried on that day, so once again I will stay positive, and one more thing I will sees Peter and I also will sees him for thanksgiving.

Well I am still talking about my boyfriend, and he just doesn't have time for me and he said he is always busy and so he just doesn't have time. And then he comes in like 3 am and then he goes to sleep and then he stay out alls night and seems like he does not care about me, maybe I repeat this before but I think it is true, and that is no lies.

My friend Delores told me to drop him, and he is the wrong type of man that only thinks about myself and he does not care for anyone he were be here for me, well I don't wants to change him. Also I don't be change neither; well I will let him be. I know he will realize that I am the best thing in his life and he doesn't know how to care for, unless I scare him and says that I cannot do this.

But I think that probably were not work neither and he doesn't listen to me but I just have to listen to his crisis and my don't matter, but thing at not exact good at this time for me, but they will be better.

I guess I let him to use me like a floor mat from the first day I met him and I think that was a totally mistake and he is just that type of man that act like a jerk sometime and I don't want to be that ways but sometime I have no choice in the matter, so did my boyfriend took me on a weekend trip and the answer is no but I did and he didn't have worry about anything but Peter being on the computer and not paying to me.

I thought that was rude and sometime he think that I am a mind reader but I am not.

So I am patience person and I do get along with peoples and I am person that understand and care for peoples, but he told me that he was abuse when he was a child so that why he is this ways and but I think that I should not make excuses for Peter, well but I am still happy that I am with him and I know that everyone is not prefect and I know I do have my fault but not has much has his so, and life is too short to complains, and now I don't want to sound selfish and I don't think about myself but other peoples too.

About Me

There are days that I feel alone but I know that I am not, I have my mom and my brother and sister and two nephews,, well I don't sees a lot of my sister because she has her family to take care and she is also a nurse.

But you know that I am writer and I work on my book and my last book was published and it is called "SPOOKY" and it was publish by Publish America. I was very happy about that and I also have more horror and ghostly books and called Willow Lakes haunting and mysterious night and night of terror, and those were self publish. But I know that I have fan and I was at the Millrace Bookstore, in Farmington, Connecticut and the owner is Jane and she is very nice lady and so let me tell you about March 7, 2010, I was first in the Hartford Courant, saying that I were be there, and one of my fan was from Manchester and I bought two books that he purchase online, Thin Ice Zombies in LA Nowhere to Hide and NO Ending Dreams and I signed for him and that was awesome.

That was a great experience to have when you are the author and you have a fan to comes out and sees you, and I was happy about that's so that was the first time it happen and one other incident happened at the big e last year.

But this year at the Big e my two books got lost or stolen or sold and that was the first time and I was surprise that never happened to me but with other peoples, and I hope that I were get money for those books and that is unfair, because I didn't lose them, and I believe that whoever were in possession during the big e and that there responsible for the books.

Because I gave 20 books and they sold about 19 book but include 3 missing I believe that I should get paid, and I am honest person and I believe that I should not be cheating out and lost of my three books. But

I don't blame Delores and Mark but they were the one that were running the store, and other CAPA member. Says if I was rich, I still were wants for the loss of the books, but I am not rich and this incident happen and that is not my fault so they should pays for the loss of the books.

That were be fair and honest ways of do it and then I were make a big deal out of it but it is and I don't have money to misplace these books and if I did it were not be fair, because I should get what was loss and make at the big e.

Well that how I feel a bit angry and sometime I think that peoples are making fun of me and two members CAPA think that I am smart and something wrong with me and I don't like that I am normal and no one should treated you that ways, and that is not normal person if they do that.

I feel alls my life I was laughed at and put down, listen I do have feeling and I do know what going on and something I think should be left alone.

I am normal just like you, and but why treated that your not?

Sometime I feel alone and have no one to talk too.

Then sometime I feel a little depressant, but I don't need too, and that probably cause stress and then it occurs to have vertigo and then I am being trap in my house and unable to drive because I feel that I do have some kind of disability, because unable to drive to the store or go to the bank and go and sees my sister and take out my mom out and let her sees more than four walls in the house.

My mom likes to stay home and then she tells my brother to take her to the cemetery to see my dad and talked with him but I don't think that today my mom will not go and see the grave today.

But maybe on Saturday my mom might go to the firehouse for the pasta to help the fireman to the fundraiser, but I know that I will be going with Barbie, and that is October 23, and about 4 pm that day but in the morning I will go with my brother to get rid of the old paints and then we will go home and maybe to the vet to pick up heart worm medication for Susie.

But why do I feel so alone when I am with my mom and I cannot explains it and I do miss my dad whole lot and I wish that we help him out but we couldn't help him and now he is gone it will be going on four month in November 5, 2010. I know that I am repeating myself but I need to stop about the loss of my dad and I know I am not the only one that loss a dad and life goes on and you need to be strong and that alls I need to says.

So yesterday my sister called and said her and her husband that they have a bad cold and so far that she know that the stone is not place yet for my dad so that is the fault at the cemetery worker and some got let go.

But about my friend Delores got really mad and because I told the boss about the incident that happened and I thought he knew but he didn't know and he forward the email to Delores and she got pissed and said I make it worst but how when she told me that he knew what she was trying to do snow job and then think that the (retard) would not do anything and I am also not the troublemaker if they watched it I would complain and this is the first time ever happen and I don't like it and they were not paying the attention, I believe I really don't want to belong to this associate because they think they are too and I am stupid and then about couples member don't even speak to me and think they are above and beyond and then they think that I am not normal and I don't like that.

The day of the restaurant, they were making fun of me and not too my face but the expression and I didn't like it and they thought that I didn't notice it and so called friend "Delores" I thought she was my friend but she like stab my back and put me down and when my dad passing way she kind of ways coming over here less and telling me to get rid of my boyfriend, well my boyfriend, they have the same birthday and sometime there personality are the same. And I don't understand why she just got angry; I think that she didn't report it and she just got angry.

Yesterday I spoke with Barbie and I hope that she will be going to Worcester to Peter and Dante, the reason that she gave that if Ed does not have a day off, she is not going well if you make plan you should go even though if your husband don't go, so I hope that you agree with me.

Today my mom called the social security and they had the wrong date of her birthday, well they will fix it. But it will not be a problem with the benefit.

When they apply I guess my mom told them the wrong date.

I am not worry so I believe everything is fine and today I think that my brother, will get rid of the garden and then he will rake the leaves and then put them into the bag and then it will be done and then I think that my brother will wash the clothes and then hang up and then later watched the movie that he order from Neflix, and that is a good service.

Now I will be watching the Rachel Ray show and it is a good program and I were like to be her guest on her show, but I hope this year I will hit national.

Right now I will not think about it and so I know that my mom is doing fine and last night I didn't have no more nightmare, and now I am dealing with my dad death, much better and there are moment that I wants to cried, but I hold it in and I cannot says anymore about my loss and I was daddy girl and he was the only one that listen to me and he was the best dad and I do love him very much, and I do miss my dad each morning.

So you need to know I do trust my friends but they treated me like I am nothing and they are rude and means and tell me out and said that I am going to died if I don't start doing thing but I do have a problem just like this morning when I walks my dog and I was weak and I was worry that I might fall and I don't know what going on with me and it happened last Feb, and the vertigo hit and I still trying to recover from this and I when to ears and nose doctor and told me that I got crystal in my ears and I never heard of that and I was surprise and now I have to live with it and I don't know why I am being punish, and I am a good person and I do have fault but everyone else does too.

Sure I do want to help my brother out and I do want to do chores like going to the store and pick up some items with my mom or even alone to Stop and shop I am willing to tried but today I notice that I am not strong and my friend Delores make me cried and got me stress and I believe that cause this to happen to me and I don't like this and I wish it were be gone and I even pray to god and so far it is not working, but I know I will get stronger.

The only three friends Karen, and Barbie and Donna they do care for me.

True Friends

Yes my best friends I bet Barbie in school in New Britain, Connecticut and I met Karen after when Gary passed away and we did have argument with each other but then we were fine and then I talked with Donna but I have not met her yet! I need to says my male friends are Joe that lives in West Palm and he is always with me and he talked with me about my problem and then I have friend that live in Windsor and with his parents but he is having a lot problem right now and he said he were contact me and we would sees each other soon but his dad is not doing that good and then it my boyfriend Peter that lives in Worcester and I do talked with him but he is very busy and I don't know what he is doing and I would really like to have him close but someday we will and I sometime he is means and rude like Delores.

Well I don't want to talked about Delores, and I don't how it will work out between us now and she blame me for the mess that I that I make I don't think so, she cause the problem and not me so let skip this one right now.

Yes I do like Barbie and ED and Karen and Donna and Ricky and they are good and they don't talked behind my back and not Peter neither and back to Delores she really hate Peter and she told me to get rid of him and he can be dangerous, but I don't understand, she has a little bad personality herself and I know that she is not perfect and I am not neither but she got on my case and I thought she was my friend and I guess she fool me, and back to the incident when I fell she saw me about to fall why she didn't catch me, I guess she didn't care, and I think that I got fool.

Because I trust the wrong persons in my life and that is totally wrong and I will know better, but also I will not feel sorry for myself or I don't want peoples to be pity on me and I hate that's! So I will take one day at the time and then I know that I will sees Karen in November and I will sees my boyfriend and we will, Do things and it will be fun and I hope the weather will be nice and I will think about it now, it is October 22, 2010 and so far I didn't hear from my friend that got angry and hung up the phone for no reason at alls, and I believe I didn't do anything, and it is all her fault and not mine. Ok went you have friends you gets along and then sometime you do disagrees but you don't get furious, and get mad and swear, at them and then they wander why you don't called them well they should treated you like dirt and like you don't know anything and you stupid or something and that is not nice, and I were never do that to anyone, and think that they are smarter than you and you should apply for some kind of benefit. Like a retard and you are not and so I think her you are not normal and I just don't like it not at alls. But I do need to think about staying in that group, but right now I am not sure that I wants to stay, they think that they are smarter than you are.

Friends that you thought you trusts.

Well I find out the hard way I make a mistake and reporting that couples items were missing to the boss and I thought she was my friend, she got pissed about me telling the boss about me I should have got pissed because she didn't do anything about it and said I doubt it that you will gets your money, and it probably will comes out of my pocket, at that time I couldn't get through and she hung up the phone, and I did send her email and apology even though it was not my fault she should have apology to me I didn't do anything to her. I don't know why she is making me has the bad guy when I didn't do anything to her, but she did too me.

I tried to explains and the first thing that she said you really pissed me off and I don't like it and stop crying I don't care if you do cry and it will not help, well this was my first time of my lost and she is acting like it is a federal case, big deal, and I am not the only one did lost the item, so what wrong with her? I would understand if I said this every year but I didn't and now she is acting like a bitch, and I don't deserve that's! She is not better than I am, but it seems like she think she is.

Well I will not called and get reject because of her bad attitudes and also don't have peoples manner and well if they get your nervous, well I think you shouldn't do it and if you cannot act like an professional, so gets out of the business, and don't be pissed and angry for no reason at alls.

The point is that in the first place that I told the boss I thought he knew and she lied to me because she told him about someone else items and not mind and I think that she thought that I were just swept under the carpet and think that I am not normal and were not says anything, I am stupid and I was not born yesterday and I did trust her but she told me too many stories and I don't if it happened to her and I guess she were not like it neither.

Well the weekend is over and so far I have not heard from her and I think I didn't get her in trouble but she didn't like that I told Barbie, but I tell Barbie about the event every year I do and I just told her that three items were missing or misplace at this point she is not talking to me and no ways in hell that I will called and beg her but her fault in the first place of stalling me.

These days it is tough to know who you can trust and you really your friend.

I guess I think you need to know that person, I don't want to judge her but I believe that she just turned on me and I guess she doesn't want to bother with me because I am not really the type that just jump on something and make them feel bad and hurt so I think that she did that too me and I don't know if I am willing to forgive her for being so rude and means to me, I didn't tell anyone in the group what happen but to the boss and she just blew me out of the water. So what do think about my friend? But Delores is my friend and we talking and this is like therapy what happens and so everything is ok between us and so she will understand that the only ways I could put in writing and we both were mad and everything is fine.

New Project

Ok now it is time to focus, and not swell about friends that says that they love you and a minute later they hang up on the phone and being nasty and rude and means to you, I don't need being treated that ways from anyone that even says that she cares but that is the strange ways of showing it.

Now back to my new project well soon I will be having my own talked radio on the internet, after I finish my book and I will be working on book 26 and then also I will have the talk radio and I will be the host and I will have caller and my fans will follows what new with me and what coming up like a book signing event and then I will have guest on my show and I will be talking about movies and music and maybe I will asked my friend Erik Narwhal being a guest on my show and he can talked about his music and what going on with his band, Erik Narwhal and the Manatees, and how I met him and how he promote me at the Foxwoods casino and he told his friends and I know that I do have followers with my books, and that is really awesome and meeting Mickey Dolenez at the Big E that was great and giving him my pen and being my friend on Face book and that is really great and also I help out with the March of Dimes and I donation my books and for the fundraiser and also for MS. I am a kind and friendly person and I do get along with peoples. And I don't understand that why peoples treated me this ways?

I also planned to go Connecticut school of broadcasting for more of studio time and maybe I will be someday on Tic 96.5 and that is really awesome and my dreams. I am sure if I am going to help with the Gary Craig with the Christmas party but time will tell and the organize is called we are the children, and I did that couples times and it was great and it was location at the expo center in Hartford and I will probably give a donation of some kind of amount and I think that would be a good thing to do.

But no promises but now I need to set up the phone and the computer and get ready to be on air and I will have a lot to says and it will be a positive show and I will says positive and I hope that I will have a lot listeners and hope that I will make a name for myself, and no one is helping me, and about more than 8 month ago I gave Delores and she didn't work on it but when it was someone else she did do the work and I told her that I were pays her but she just kind came up that she was busy but doing other stuff for other peoples and I thought it was unfair.

Maybe I am complaining but I have the right and I thought the book were have been published but I guess not, I am not mad at her but I am glad that I could have a new version and I think it is better and you will know me and what make me tick, and that is a good thing I hope.

Now

Today is October 26, 2010 and everything is fine with my friends and with my boyfriend and my mom doing better and yesterday my mom and brother when to the cemetery to sees my dad and so far my dad does not have his gravestone still and I don't think that it will be ready for soul days that is on Halloween day and it will be crowded and difficult parking so I will sees if we are going to light the candle for my dad that day, but time will tells.

I really don't like going to the grave, and I do miss my dad in November will be four month of his passing. But by now you should know that I am was very close to my dad and so I really, really miss him and it is not the same, about this time he were be doing the leaves outside and then he were do the kitchen floor and help out my brother, because my mom unable to do work like that "doctor order" and I am not strong and I do have my moment that I do get worry so, now my brother has too do thing by himself, and I know it is unfair but I am not strong.

My mom were like to help but she cannot, so he does almost of the chores and my mom and I make dinner and we wash the dishes and change the bed and maybe we will do the laundry, and so we will take it slowly.

Today I took my dog Susie out and I was worry and but I am ok, and yesterday I spoke with Karen and Delores and Peter, and Peter has his friend from Maine and he told me that his friend gave him a nasty message on his and said you don't care about yours girlfriend "Jean" and he told me that I said I don't remember when I spoke to her, I said about five days, but I could be wrong.

Then I spoke to Delores and told me that Mark will be home today and so she will be unable to call me but we are fine and I did apology, and I will let that go, and leave in the past.

I think that my sister probably will come over today but I hope not.

But I did feel sorry about my mom because my mom missed my dad a lot and I cannot explain, so it will never be the same in this house.

But I know that I need to cope with this and I know that my dad were not want us to cry nonstop, so life goes on and my mom still bring it up what happen and but we try to save my dad but it was too late, because of that massive stroke that destroy his brain and filled with blood, but my dad was a great man and kind man and good to us, in good and bad times we had foods and clothes and we were very happy and we were not poor but were middle class, and every holiday we had everything and I do remember this day.

My dad was a hard worker and he loved his family and we were never abuse, but loved my mom and dad, and he was a wonderful parent and we are going to miss him very much.

Now you can tell that I have a big heart and I am friendly and caring person, but I am not saying that I am not perfect, and I do have fault.

I know after finishing this book I will be working with my new book and it will be horror and it will be for young adult and I should says I do like to write and I do want to accomplish my goal and then I will be on air and my friend will help me out on this week and I will have a talk radio show and I will build my recognize and then more fans, and I would like to meet them alls, and I an ordinary girl and I do gets along with everyone.

Yes I need to says I cannot wait to sees my boyfriend in November and I wander who going but so far I know that Barbie going and I hope Ed too and so time will tell, well I just wants to says that life goes on and I will be around and hope that you enjoy my book and you can find me on my website and I am also on Face book and I am on twitter and so I am working on many project and you will be able to find out what I will be doing and what will be coming and then I need to says I that I am not too happy right now I bit down like under the weather, but I will be fine.

So let me tell you about the polish Christmas in my house, first we looked for dry mushroom for the cabbage soup and then we have pirgoies, and then pickles herring and rye bread and bake potatoes, and wafer, and that is alls and on Christmas eve we open the Christmas presents, and then we go to my sister house and I know that my boyfriend is included but what he did last year I hope that he is welcome to her house.

But back to Peter friends in New Haven, Peter make her mad because he does not shown up and that get her pissed and I don't blame her not all.

About my sister always bring up life insurance, about my dad well that not her business well, says if my dad had it belong to my mom not her, that how I feel, so it is always money in her mind and she also didn't give us time to breathe and we told her that we didn't have the money and my mom was really confuse and it really too fast, ok I hope that I am going over and over, and my friend Joe that live in Florida he wants to sees my boyfriend picture and I suppose to send to him so far I forgot and so I will do it later and I think that he like Karen and I think that Karen known, and so that does not matter, and sometime dealing with men it is a pain in the ass.

Because they acted like little boys so I hope you agree with me so I really open up about myself and I hope that I didn't says too much. My family will go on without my dad and I will be seen the holiday will not be the same without my dad.

The holiday will not be the same because my dad will not be at the head of the table anymore and he will be missed by everyone and now I need to says that my sister mention the funeral and she got stuck with the bill and once again I need to says that we told her that we couldn't afford and she got the more expensive place that we couldn't afford it but my sister pick but my listen didn't listen to us ok I have talked this in my other chapter.

Today my mom and I try to do the wash but the water was mix and we couldn't do it and so we just left it alone.

Yesterday I heard from my friend, Ricky and he told me about his parents and that he is the only, doing everything for his parents and his do not nothing and that is unfair, and I said I know about his situation.

Then he said that we might go rolling skating and then we when to the free spirit and dance for a while, that night.

But two night ago spoke with Peter friend and she kept me on over two hours and she has a lot of problem, so I listened to her and told me that my boyfriend has skeleton in the closet and refuse to tell me but I know that I need to know the dark secrets of my boyfriend and I don't why she haven't told me so now I am wandering what it is? Hope that he is not a child predator or rapist and even worst a serial killer that really terrifies me. Also I want apologize bad mouth my friends that how I felt, but I just said what I felt at that time.

You should understand went you just say what on your mind, but I was being rude just thinking loud, I do to apology to my friends.

Today is October 28, 2010 and we talking about the Mohegan sun casino, if went there I would if I won I would take the winning and don't look back and use it for money for something else.

Well, today I am doing well and my mom is better, also my brother too, my dog just turned 8 years. She does miss my dad. But now thing have changed and I really don't like but you do need to move and not sulk on the past and the holiday and being the family will lives on and that will never change.

But I know that my brother and I got along with my dad much better, but my mom is a different story and she gets along with my sister and she does not hear that well and my father said that she should get a hearing aid.

You need to repeat couple times to understand what we are saying, I yelled at her and she doesn't like it but I have no choice and sometime she doesn't understand, but she is 85 year old but she doing well, but problem with her feet, but the doctor don't help and she suffering and cannot walks.

But the doctor doesn't care about old patience but only the money.

SECRETS

I know that everyone has dark secrets, some are big and some are small.

Now I will be talking about my boyfriend, what do I know about him not much, he keeps me in the dark, I don't anything about him and he goes places and leave about 6 pm and comes back to my house at 3 am and he didn't tell me where he is.

What else is he hiding me, am I danger from him I don't know.

I need to know what make him tick and what are his "secrets" if I ever marry him or being with him I need to know.

But he is not open and honest with me. That only ways that I will be with him and I don't like secrets and I am not the one keeping them but he is like a mysterious man, that I ever met and I think that Peter should take me about his past and his friend Donna known and why am I out in the cold and would like to know and then if we have a future and I don't want any surprises from his past to haunted me so I will asked him about his past and if he does not tell me I need to asked Donna and promise that I would not tells Peter that she told me. But if I find out that his secret might hurt me I might just end the relationship and probably were be safe in my case and also Peter does stupid thing like going into bad neighbor and get into trouble and then he helped out boys that don't have home,. So that seems a bit off and I think that the boys can take care of themselves and they don't need Peter guidance.

They are adult and they do have family some of them but that is not his concern,, so he said that he wanted me to move in with him but I am not going too, because he always has company over and one of them might steal my cell phone or money and I were not feel comfortable there at that time.

But seeing him at his friend house like Dante, sure I guess that is fine but not with the crowds, I really were not be my best interest of doing that.

But you need to know something that really scared me went he is mister nice guy and then he turned into mister bad guy and he start yelling and screaming and no reason at alls. But he does and I wander if he was abuse by a parent when he was a child and now I think that I am analyze him and I don't want to put in more than what is really., and he also tell stories and sometime I don't know if they are true or just in his mind.

Some stories you need to think and says are they are true and most of the times they probably are.

But I am thinking to myself sure I am with Peter over four years but he really didn't come to me but if he did comes then he think and then he says I have a appointment and then he retuned about in the early morning and you wander where he had gone and what have he been doing all that night.

Before he comes he called me on my house phone and said make sure that you let me in and meanwhile he woke up my parents and my dad was not too thrill about Peter, there would moment that my dad did like him but there moment that some how my dad dislike him. So Peter was getting better with my family and then he messed up and then they again dislike him.

I do understand about the panic disorder attack, and being paranoid, one night Peter stay in my home and I slept on the couch and I forgot something in my room, but he lock it and I needed to go inside and he freak out but he should understand that is my room and not his.

Then there was an other incident that my brother and I went for pizza and Peter arrival he rang the doorbell and my mom answered and then he just walk inside and walks toward the living room and sat down and didn't says anything to my dad and put his feet up and then I came home and I saw his car and then I walks up to him and he said that he was tired and so I can go to your room because I am tired, and at that time I think that he when to visit his mom, but he still keeps things to himself.

I am trying to say dating Peter and it is hard to read him but I am still with him and one of these days I am going to find out his secrets.

But I hope they are not bad but I hope that I could deal with them because I know that I am strong lady and I know I am able to do that's!

Long times ago I also had panic attack and I stay home and I did have the shaking and very nervous but I also have secrets. I think that Peter don't know them but I have reveal my secret to Delores and she also told me about her, so we are honest to each other but Peter is not.

I know that being in a relationship you need to trust the person and not too have doubt about anything, and one other thing I dislike about Peter is that he make me travel and he know that I cannot drive the highway but he still want me to go to him, and I think it is unfair to me because he is more able to comes to me, than I am capable to drive on the highway because I got scare once and I thought I were have ended up in a accident but I was lucky on 84 coming back from Waterbury, but one car almost hit me but I made it home in one piece.

That happened in 1991 when I met Barbie and Billy at 25 a at the hotel when I told her about the Amway meeting and she met David but she doesn't remember him, and that was a long time ago, but it was good seeing them once in a while.

There was an other incident that I almost hit a car but I didn't and I was glad that I didn't and then at walnut hill park,, it was a close called so I have reveal my secrets, at least some of them, but Peter nothing at alls.

Well I have much more secrets but they are more like money matter but I will says more about it, it will be taking care of soon.

Mr. Wrong

I will tell you why? Well I thought if I didn't give what they wanted, they were not be my boyfriend and I thought in the past if I gave myself they were like me better and so seems like all my life I been used by men because I wanted love and affection but I was being use for sex and at that time I didn't like myself and I didn't have self esteem and I kind of didn't like myself and I was not a happy person and so I just got used by men and I thought it was love,. And I guess I didn't like myself and I was used for sex and money and also been called names and but I still stay with him.

I really thought, I was being like and not being use and I thought if I gave sex they really do like me but they were only lies to have sex with them.

I really explained why I did that one of my boyfriend that I had a addicted to sex probably I did, and time when by and I think I started to like myself better and I started to say no to sex and I somehow being like a object in those men eyes and I just understood that if a man really like you and he were not force you into sex and he were stand by you and like you but there are some dogs that just wanted sex and left and there were not the one that I were end up with, so there was a man name David and he used me for sex and money and he really use me and I then he cheat on me and hurt my heart with the other lady and so he left town and then there was Jon in Los angles and he also used for sex and money and then he asked me to marry him and then he cheat on me and then he got marry to Norma and that was the end of that's!

Then I have not heard from him and I think he is divorce by now and then I really don't care and so I have move on to a good man and now I am with him over four years and I still sees my old friend Ricky.

I hate being use and I don't understand why and because it is not written on my forehead ands so what wrong with me am I an easy target or what?

So, I am better person and I am more positive and I accomplish my goal and I do write my novel, and but too men, well I have a friend Joe and we do get along and but I had bad experience about men on the internet and they just want sex from you and don't care about your feeling, just having fun.

I believe the good men are taking and marry and most of the jerk is still available, and I am sure that I don't want to deal with them.

I didn't have a lot men but they were user and so I cannot explains why I couldn't have a honest man that were love me and be with me and spend time with me well my boyfriend Peter, but he seem to busy for me but a lot time for his male friend he does have time and I believe that he should be for me and I am not being selfish, but seem like he is for me and he should know that I need him now more than ever.

What is Peter keeping what kind of secrets and why don't he tell me I were like to know but I don't understand why he is like that ways maybe he was abuse when he was a child by a parent, but ,my mom says why do you get the wrong man in your lie why can you have a nice guy is here for you and this is never around when you need the most and I don't understand and you are a pretty girl and I don't understand, but I try explain I really didn't know what to says and I said I know but so I always stuck with mister wrong and all my life and I am not saying that Peter is Mister wrong but he should be here with me now but he just hang out with his friend and I don't count it seem like it but, I am sure but he does called, well my friend Ricky is here more for me than my boyfriend Peter, and don't sees the picture that my friend has time for me and about my boyfriend he does not.

When my dad passed away my friend Ricky was here for me and my boyfriend couldn't handle It., but I believe he should have been here and but he was not.

So I need to says what wrong with me, well I have long platinum blonde and I am about five feet and one inches tall and I have blonde and blue eyes and I am a bit overweight and then I have a nice personality and I am peoples person and I gets along and I think that I am not tough and that why peoples walk over me and treated me badly and I am not the type that I don't get mad, but I think that I am soft and that is not good.

I believe that I have a bad side but not strong enough and I think that

I am a strong person in someway and there the other ways I am weak and I believe that everyone like control me and I don't like that even though and I am not a teenager anymore I should says that I am in my fifty and I still treated like a child from my mom and my brother and sister and in the past my dad too.

I guess being a baby in the family and just being treated like a baby and I think I have not grown up but I have and so is my mind and I know how to take care of myself and I do know how to take care of the financial and but still some peoples think that my brother take care of everything, so on my forehead says Retard, and I don't think so maybe I am a little slow but that does not means that I don't know anything, but I do know thing like making my own website and now BLOG radio show and I know some peoples don't know how to do website and then link there website to other so bad to men think that I am stupid and I don't know anything they don't.

Also I hate when someone put a label on you and they are no better than you are. So whoever you meet and they tried to put down but don't let them get down and positive and put your head up and be a happy person.

Sure being in relationship, you need to trust the one that your involve.

I do know love this man and I don't know where it going to take me.

November 1 2010

Day before election of course I will vote and it is very difficult decision to make, I started to vote went I was 18 year old and they I was under age kid wanted to vote so had show my id and then I voted.

But tomorrow my friend Ricky will be coming over and I don't what we are going to do.

But my mom and brother doesn't know that he is coming and I am going to pretend that it is a surprise, because my brother is not too crazy about him and then about Peter they don't like him neither.

Well I need to mention, that will be four month of my father death and so we alls missed him, but meanwhile my brother is drinking a lot of brandy and beers and because he really missed him very much.

But life goes on and I will make a better life and I will live my life.

I know each days will be better, but my mom still cried for my dad and my mom not going so good because she missing him so, so, much.

If we know how to save my dad probably he would be here but I think he would be maybe that night we should have took him to the hospital.

I wander if we did but I know it is too late, so maybe I cannot deal with it maybe that why it is hard for me because I was very close to him.

So far I didn't really cried hard but I know I need to let go.

Now I am talking to Delores and talking about Halloween to mark parent's house and Delores make the meal.

I don't understand why didn't cook for them, and unfair.

Later today I will be washing the clothes and helping my mom.

Later I will make lunch and probably will go to the cemetery.

But time goes by and we will be all fine, but I will keep on writing.

I will keep my dreams alive and I am not going anywhere but just being successful. Ands hit the national and being known and being friends with movie stars and Donald trump, that would be nice and being on his show, and show. That my dreams, I hope it will happen.

Well the election came and went and my friend came over and stays over and we had a stuff pizza, he had seven pieces. Ricky and I watched "dancing with stars". Then we a little election and then we watched the horror flick the house on haunted hill, and Ricky was scare and felt the chill on his back.

Then he started to called names, and I don't like that.

Then Peter called but I didn't answer because a lot he doesn't neither.

But I have not heard from him and I know I will soon and today my mom is not feeling well but I am worry about her and that she is fine so doesn't even comes over and seeing her how she doing?

I am the only one that care for my mom, sure my brother helped out sometime. But I am the only that really care for my mom with the medicine.

Today is November 3, 2010 and nothing exciting, and I will be going to bank and then to the cemetery to gets the candle and bring them home.

Then my brother will make chicken on grill and Marconi with vegetable and that will be delicious.

Later that day I will make lunch for my mom and I and hot tea.

Then I will be watching a polish soap opera and it is called "PLENBIA ".

PLENBIA is a parish and my mom really enjoy that show, I also will watched my soap opera I do enjoy, but I am really exciting about having my own talk radio and I will be talking about my books and music and movies, and I will gets notice and be popular, but I will give the best what I have and I don't want no pity from anyone or being a laughed at and having my feeling hurt.

I am Jean Marie Rusin, and I did accomplished my dreams and I am not going anywhere, and I will be around and I will have more books published, and I know after this book I will be working on a new fiction horror book that will be scary and blew your sock, but at this time I didn't decided on the title but it will be published later date 2011.

So hope that you enjoying reading my book?

So I am live and kicking and I am in good health and I have a good life and I have no complains, about anything I am in love with Peter and I know that I will sees him soon; well I am not saying bye but hello.

This is not the end but the beginning of more about me in the future.

I am establish author and I also when to broadcasting, I really enjoy doing behind the scene and being the talent so you can find me in face book and twitter and I will be your friend and I will listen to your advice.

So talk with you soon, I will be here for a long time.

HAPPY THANKSGIVING AND MERRY CHRISTMAS AND HAPPY NEW YEAR! More books will be published by Jean Marie Rusin. And listen to her talked radio show about alls topics.

Hope that I don't feel confuse and stupid and how some peoples treated me like I don't know anything at alls, but I am normal like you are.

Also I do have feeling and I don't want to be a laughing stock., I am only human, so I will still keeps on writing and I do enjoy it very much.

Thanks for reading my book and I believe you will know the real me after you read this book. I am just human and I do have feeling.

So I will survive and the present time of my life is that it is like over a year ago that my dad passed away and things are different and I do miss my dad and my brother went to the hospital, check his colon and he does not have cancer and on the day that he went, something happened that I suddenly got sick, when I read the paper that my brother got and about bleeding that day, I almost passed out and so I think that I just got a panic attack and ever since that day, I am feeling fine and I also have glaucoma and I am doing fine and this year I when to the Big E and I did good sales with my books and still going on and tomorrow I am going to have lunch with Karen at Town and country, and what I said before about my friends, but Delores and is my best, best, friend, what I said means stuff, I was only angry and I didn't means it, and I am very sorry and you dear too me and you the best and I do care.

I do love you are just like my sister but you much closer too me.

I lives with my mom and my brother, and we get along fine and I did go through a lot in my life and one more thing I wants to says I will continue writing and I will not stop, my dreams. Now I am working on the sequel (Thin Ice Zombies in LA) nowhere to run or hide! Battle and it will be coming soon!!! Hope that you enjoy my story, and have a wonderful day!

Apology to my friend, Delores, yes I was bad about the incident about the event and lost of items, and but I didn't means to says what I says I am very sorry, when I was writing this book, and I was still upset and I hope that you will know that I do care for you a whole lot and you did help me when I needed it and maybe should have said what I said in the book, but at that moment was mad and I believe when someone is mad at someone they should keep to themselves, and I want too apology, and overacting at that moment and writing that email, but you are my best, true friend, I apology being a jerk, hope that you forgive me for writing in this book of my story and it was just not thinking at that moment of time, I am very, very, very, sorry my dearest friend, Delores, and I do love you has sister and sorry bad mouth you in the book, but I didn't means it. Love you Delores very much and dear too me, if I didn't have you in my life, no one does not care has much has you for me, and taking me to the doctor and places and getting me better, you are the best. Your dearest friend Jean Marie Rusin, always! I wants to says to my mom, I live with her and I wants to says that she is very important too me and I love you mom, always, and I miss dad a lot and I think of dad alls the time, I miss you very much! You are in my heart and we will always remember you dad, and we will never forget you and love you!

JEAN MARIE RUSIN, lives with her mom and brother, in New Britain, CT, Jean Marie Rusin, member of Connecticut Authors and Publishers Association, and Jean Marie Rusin, graduation from Connecticut School of Broadcasting, September 7, 2007, and Jean Marie Rusin, have Talk radio and I am also on Twitter, My space, and on Face book, Jean Marie Rusin, Fan club CT and Jean Marie Rusin, Branch in Michigan, and my website is www.jeanmarieruisn.com , and my email is jrusin31@yahoo.com to contact me, hope too hears from you.